SELF DELIVERANCE

Manual

Dr. Sebenke Simon

© 2020

ACKNOWLEDGEMENTS

My gratitude goes to; God the Father, God the Son and God the Holy Spirit for the wisdom, grace and revelation He gave to me to write this MANUAL.

I am mindful of the unparalleled love, prayers, support and patience of my darling wife Buendasi Simon and our children, Brother Pako Jens and Sister Boipelo Ludo.

To Prophet T. Kgaodi who co-laboured with me in the delivery of this manual and the household of S.G.M for their support and prayers.

I would also like to thank The Altar Media Publisher for partnering with me in bringing my messages into literature to world.

WARNING

Self-Deliverance is not for sinners. Sinners must repent, give their lives to Jesus Christ and be born again. If you are a sinner do not attempt to conduct Self-Deliverance.

Before you begin the process of deliverance from evil spirits; first you must be delivered from the power of sin. As already mentioned, this can be done by first giving your life to Jesus and having Him as your Lord and personal saviour (John 3:3; Romans 3:23; 6:23; 2 Corinthians 5:17).

Contents

CHAPTER 1
WHAT IS DELIVERANCE?

It is being set free from spiritual bondages and barriers that hold you back from walking in the victory that Jesus won for you on the cross (Colossians 2:14, John 19:30; Genesis 3:15;1 John 3:8).

HOW DEMONS GAIN ACCESS IN A PERSON'S LIFE

There are many ways demons can gain access into a person's life. This can be through vows, covenants, disobedience etc. The main door for demons to enter is sin. When you do Self - Deliverance, you need to know how demons entered your life. This is the most important part of deliverance. It is important to know what opened the door for them to enter so that after casting them out you can close the door.

Some people criticise deliverance but listen, nobody can stop deliverance because it is of God and it is Him who commanded it to be done (Acts 10:38-39).

If at all you want to be free from demons you must be ready to fight for your life (Matthew 11:12). Spend as much time as you can in the presence of God before your deliverance. Obeying the word of God and doing what He tells you to do gives you the right to use His name and to ask whatever you want in His name (Luke 6:46-49). Jesus Christ wants you to use His name to take authority over demons and their father satan. He has given you the power to overcome the kingdom of satan.

PREPARATION FOR SELF DELIVERANCE

1. Identify areas of your life that need deliverance (John 5:6-9)

Make a list of things in your life that you want to get rid of e.g. anger, bitterness, lust, unforgiveness, stinginess, selfishness, satanic dreams, pride etc.

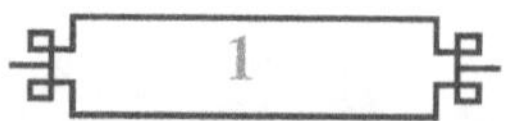

2. *Be desperate*

Be desperate and be determined to be delivered. You must be ready to fight for your life (Matthew 11:28; 11:12). Your seriousness must be seen.

3. *Make restitution*

Restitution is an act of amending wrongs done against our fellowmen, restoring stolen or misappropriated things to their rightful owners, paying back debts, making confession to the offended and apologizing to those slandered (Hebrews 4:13; Acts 24:16).

4. *Prayer and fasting*

Prayer and fasting help in preparation for deliverance. It builds our faith (Matthew 17:21).

5. Forgive

Forgive those who have hurt you so that the father may forgive you too (Mark 11:25). You cannot be forgiven if you do not forgive.

SELF DELIVERANCE PROCEDURE

1. Get a quiet place where there is no disturbance. Any convenient place where you can pray and not be disturbed will be fine.
2. Sanctify the place and declare it holy ground.
3. Repent and forsake all your sins (1 John 1:9).
1. Ask God to forgive you all your sins, depart from them and receive salvation from Jesus Christ. You must hate sin. Make a complete and total surrender to Jesus Christ. Genuine, godly sorrow leads (2 Cor 7:9-11) to repentance (Romans 10:9-10; John 5:14).
4. Cover yourself with the blood of Jesus Christ (Revelations 12:11)
5. Create an atmosphere conducive for deliverance through praise and worship
2. (Psalms 46:10; 63:6). Spend much time in the presence of God. Worship God in Spirit and truth (John 4:23).
6. Pray in the Spirit.

7. Confess out loud scriptures that speak about deliverance.
8. Ask God to release angels of deliverance and war to come and assist you. Do not pray to angels, (Daniel 10:1-21; Zechariah 3:2; Jude 1:9)
9. Lie down and put your hands upon your belly – Continue praying in the Spirit.

Start your deliverance that is confronting them and compelling them out of your life.

10. Break covenants, vows, agreements and curses to destroy legal grounds. Bind evil spirits associated with the legal grounds and cast them out.
11. Forcefully and aggressively command the demon/demons to come out of your life. Call them by their names (demon of anger, a demon of lust, demon of fornication etc.) (Mark 16:17).
12. Command them by faith in the name of Jesus Christ.
13. Meditate and pray silently (Mark16:18).
14. They may try to resist but you have to drive them out forcefully and aggressively by faith.

SIGNS OF DEPARTURE OF EVIL SPIRITS

The signs of departure are tears, coughing, laughing, nose running, sneezing, screaming, body vibration/shaking etc. These are some of the signs that you might see when demons are leaving. One can begin to cough, sneeze or laugh etc.

After demons have left;

- [ ] Cover yourself with the blood of Jesus Christ
- [ ] Declare all gates that demons used to enter your life closed
- [ ] Ask God to fill you with Holy Ghost Fire

CAUTION

If the demon(s) become violent, stop the exercise. Command them to stop. Then seek help from others who can be able to cast them out.

HOW WILL YOU KNOW THAT YOU ARE DELIVERED?

You will know that you are delivered and free by not doing the evil or bad things you used to do. Close the session with prayer and thanksgiving unto the Lord.

HOW TO MAINTAIN YOUR DELIVERANCE

- Get rid of all traces of sin in your life
- Be Holy (1 Peter 1:15-16).
- Abide in the word (Matthew 4:4; Psalms 119:105).
- Constant prayer and fasting
- Sin no more
- Resist satan (James 4:7-8).
- Close all doors that satan can use to gain re-entry into your life (Luke 11:24-26, 1 Peter 5:8, John 10:10).
- Attend church regularly (Hebrews 10:25)
- Serve God

CHAPTER 2
DEALING WITH ADAMIC NATURE

Below is a list of some of the things that you might need to be delivered from.

DELIVERANCE FROM THE SPIRIT OF JEALOUSY

This can cause a lot of damage in the life of an individual and in the ministry if it is not dealt with properly. This spirit causes ungodly competitions and striving. Gossip and bitterness will be evident in a ministry where the spirit of jealousy exists (Numbers 5:14; 2 Corinthians 10:12-13). One of the main causes of jealousy is 'Insecurity'. People who are insecure about themselves are people who have jealousy towards others. Example; Sister X can be jealousy at Sister K, simply because she feels that Sister K sings better than her and she might be appointed to be a praise team leader and now because of insecurity she becomes jealous at sister K. This will invite other evil spirits like gossip, hatred, anger etc. And sister X will begin to gossip and hate sister K because of jealousy, that is why sometimes in the church you have some people hating others, backbiting and gossiping them (Proverbs 6:34; Genesis 4:4-8)? Jealousy is a demonic Spirit (Numbers 5:14, 30).

2 Corinthians 10:12, God forbids us to compare ourselves with others. Comparing ourselves to others is wrong, and if you do it, it will cause you to have a spirit of jealous. If truly you are a child of God you will know and understand that what God did for your brother, He will do for another and He will do it for you, "for there is no partiality in God" Romans 2:11.

Jealousy is pure evil. It opens doors to the demonic spirits in a person's life like no other sin. James 3:16. Jealousy inspired Cain to kill his brother Abel, Joseph's brothers to sell him to slavery and King Saul to want to destroy David. Saul's jealousy opened the door to the spirit of insanity and murder in his life. 1 Samuel 18, Genesis 37, Genesis 4:1-8.

HOW TO BE DELIVERED

- ☐ Admit that you are jealous. If you have jealousy you know it. Repent and be delivered
- ☐ Fight against it. Begin to love those you hated because of jealousy, make restitution. Learn to appreciate others. See others better than you. (Philippians 2:3)
- ☐ Refuse to be used by satan. Satan will tell you that you are better than others, he will try to put you in other people's positions. Resist him (James 4:7)
- ☐ Conduct self-deliverance. Command jealousy to come out of your life in the name of Jesus Christ. Jesus Christ said in His name we shall cast out demons (Mark 16:17). When someone is jealous they are jealous of someone else's possessions, wealth, job, achievements, success, intelligence, marriage etc.

Spirit of jealousy does not work alone; it works with other diabolic spirits like;

- ☐ **Murder**- literally wanting to get rid of the person so that you can get what they have. Saul wanted to kill David because he felt David will take his position, Cain killed Abel simply because he brought a better sacrifice than him to God. David also killed Uriah after taking Uriah's wife, Bathsheba (2 Samuel 11). A person will want to kill another one because he wants to take his wife, or it can even be for a position at work. The days we are living in are so evil in such a way that a pastor can sacrifice another one because he wants powers, he wants to be famous and popular.
- ☐ **Strife** – This is constant tensions between you and the other person and everyone else around. Some people are never at peace with anyone because of jealousy. Saul did not rest nor had peace because of David. We see these things happening in the church today whereby a brother will fight against another until he chases him away from church because of jealousy.
- ☐ **Greed/lust**- an evil desire to have what the other person have, though you have more than what they have. You will see a brother proposing every sister in the church, apart from

been controlled by lust, that's being greedy. Some people will want to be in every committee in the church because they cannot stand if they are not the ones in charge.

- ☐ **Envy**- to have what others have without any legal covenant/claim to it. (2 Samuel 11:1-27)
- ☐ **Destruction**- constantly speaking evil about the other person. Some people are always talking evil about others. They want everybody else to see this person as a very bad person. If you are always talking evil things about others, stop it, repent and be saved and ask Jesus Christ to set you free(John 8:36)
- ☐ **Competitions** - trying to compete to show others that you are better and deserve what they have.
- ☐ **Selfish ambition**- doing things not out of love for God and others but to get attention so that everyone looks at you and not the person you are jealous of.
- ☐ **Anger**- always angry at other people, even when they have not done anything that can make one angry. This anger is meant to discourage the other person, to frustrate them or confuse them so that they do not perform well in what they are to do. So that the jealous guy does it and is considered a good boy or smart boy.
- ☐ **Division**- forming quarrels in church. A jealous person will make people to fight, not to trust each other nor to live in harmony.
- ☐ **Slander**- speaking lies about a person in an attempt to destroy or damage his character
- ☐ **Striving**- working hard out of carnal motives instead of the anointing with the aim of out-doing others so that you become the centre of attraction.

EXAMPLES FROM THE BIBLE

1. **Adam and Eve** - Genesis 3

Why did Adam and Eve eat the forbidden fruit? They ate the fruit because they wanted to be like God, they were envious and greedy. They listened to the lies of the devil. They lost fellowship with God because of jealousy. Jealousy will make you lose important people in your life. Someone will come to you and advice you out of jealousy not to marry the sister you want to marry. He will tell you the sister wants you to marry her because you have money. If you listen to him, he will plant selfishness in you and you too you will be saying I don't want to marry a sister who is just after money. And after that, you will never get married. Jealousy will make you lose God's blessings. Adam and Eve lost the glory of God, they lost fellowship with God, and they died spiritually because of greediness. With all that they had from God, there was no reason why they should want to be like God.

2. **Cain and Abel** - Genesis 4. Jealous people always want something for nothing. They do not want to pay the price. They always think they have they right. God told Cain that if he does well then he shall be accepted. Some people in the church do not want to pay tithes because they are greedy, they do not want to attend prayers, they do not want to be born again but yet they want to be workers and to be involved in leadership. If they are told, you do not pay tithes therefore you cannot be a worker, they will fight their way through. Some want to continue living in sin but they want to continue singing in the worship team.

3. **Joseph's brothers**- Genesis 37-38. They hated Joseph because of jealousy. They called him names. Do not be surprised if your brethren hate you and call you names because you are faithful and loyal. Do not hate others also because they are jealous of you.

In a situation where people are jealous of you, how can you defeat this spirit?

Joseph as an example

- He forgave his brothers
- He blessed his brothers
- He gave God all the glory
- He was not prideful in his accomplishments

CONSEQUENSENSES OF JEALOUSY

- You put yourself under a curse
- Separation from God
- It becomes a generational curse- Genesis 4:24

God is a jealous God; Exodus 34:14; Joshua 24:19; Zechariah 1:14

INSTRUCTIONS

- ✓ Pray between 12 midnight to 0400 hrs. This is time to intensify prayer
- ✓ Fast from 12 midnight to 12 midnight (24 hrs.), 1-day prayer & fasting.
- ✓ During the day, also pray.

PRAYER POINTS

- ➤ Father, forgive me for my jealousies and help me to develop an attitude of gratitude in the mighty name of Jesus Christ
- ➤ Father, give me the grace to change my thoughts from that of jealousy to pure thoughts
- ➤ Forgive me for hurting and wounding your people because of jealousy, in the mighty name of Jesus Christ.
- ➤ You spirit of jealousy; I command you come out of my life in the mighty name of Jesus Christ
- ➤ I decree and declare that my conscience is purged from dead works of jealousy through the blood of Jesus (Hebrews 9:14)
- ➤ I cover my mind, conscience and thoughts with the blood of Jesus.

CONFESSION OF FAITH

I brother/sister_____________________ confess that on this______ day of _____________, I was delivered from the spirit of Jealousy and the blood of Jesus Christ bears witness to my deliverance and salvation (1 John 5:8).In the name of the Father, the Son and the Holy Spirit, amen!

ACTION: don't just pray. If you want to defeat satan and bring shame to him after your deliverance go to the brethren you were jealous of. Confess to them *"Confess your faults one to another, and pray one for another, that you may be healed. The effectual fervent prayer of a righteous man availeth much* "James 5:16. Don't keep it a secret, otherwise, it will be easy for satan to come back and take over your life again and that's why people never experience total

and permanent deliverance.

TESTIMONY: We overcome satan by the blood of the lamb and by the word of our testimony. Make sure that you testify to the glory of God and to the shame of satan. Pray for your testimony that as you testify it touches others and deliver them. Satan has been using you to fulfil his evil desires now let God use you for the expansion of His kingdom.

DELIVERANCE OF THE TONGUE

Proverbs 21:23; 18:20-21; Matthew 12:34-37

The tongue is noted as the most powerful generator of either the negative or the positive. Your life is a product of your confession. You can use your tongue to hurt, kill, and destroy or to bless (James3:1-12). Proverbs 21:23, if you want to live a peaceful life then guard your mouth and tongue. Your stomach shall be satisfied from the fruit of your mouth and the produce of your tongue so shall you be filled.

SPIRIT OF GOSSIP

Gossip is a sin that grieves the Holy Spirit. Paul the Apostle calls it corrupt communication. That is to say, this kind of communication is dead, decaying and it stinks. It is like rotten meat full of maggots. It is offensive to the spirit of God and it grieves Him. Gossip is destructive and offensive. It should not be mentioned amongst children of God (2 Corinthians 12:20).

Gossip is like a deadly poison. It hurts people, it kills relationships and it destroys trust. Gossip is usually based on hearsay. It is usually inaccurate. It creates suspicions and it divides people. It is Evil.

The Greek word for gossip means to whisper. This means that gossip almost always takes place in secret. Gossipers usually attract each other like magnets. They see things alike and therefore begin to think they are right. Don't allow the devil to use you. Make a decision today to refrain from gossip and to stay away from those who practice it. Don't gossip your brethren, rather encourage them, pray for them and talk good about them.

☐ SLANDER

To spread rumours or lies about a person to cause damage purposely (Colossians 3:8; James 4:11; Proverbs 20:19; James 5:9)

☐ RUMOURS

You hear something and it's not good and is almost not confirmed as true, but you tell someone or ask someone else about it to get more information (Proverbs 13:3).

☐ BACKBITING

It's a flavour of gossip that involves speaking slanderous words about another who is not present and can do nothing in defence (Proverbs 25:23; Psalms 101:5).

☐ MOCKERY

Proverbs 21:24; 9:8; 22:10; Psalms 1:1

☐ PLANTING SEEDS

This type of gossip is said in such a way as to make the listener have questions about the character of a person (Proverbs 16:28; Proverbs 10:19).

HORRIBLE ATTITUDES AND WRONG USE OF THE TONGUE

- ☐ Debates- church politics
- ☐ Envying- self-consumed that freely fights for self not considering the needs or desires of others. It can be translated as the word jealousy
- ☐ Wraths- deep-seated anger
- ☐ Strives- selfish desire to promote one's own way even if it means splitting or dividing the church.
- ☐ Backbiting- to speak derogatorily evil about someone else. It can be translated as the word slander.
- ☐ Whisperings- expresses the idea of a gossiper
- ☐ Swellings – it carries the idea of a person filled with pride. It can be translated to be puffed up.
- ☐ Tumults- describes the attitude or actions of a person who creates some type of disastrous disturbance.

If you have been going around using your tongue to destroy other people's lives, it is time to be delivered and stop the evil you have been doing.

How many lives have been destroyed, friends separated, how many are wounded and bleeding, how many have backslidden because of your evil tongue?

Ephesians 4:29- the word of God says corrupt communication should not proceed out of your mouth, but rather that which is good to the use of edifying, that may minister grace into the hearers. Are you the minister of grace or death? "And grieve not the Holy Spirit of God", for when corrupt communication comes out of the mouth of a believer, it causes the Holy Spirit to be grieved.

Talkative people, slanderers, gossipers, backbiters, whispers should not be allowed to be workers in the church because they grieve the Holy Spirit. 2 Corinthians 12:20, gossip is so destructive and offensive. It does not only harm people it grieves the Holy Spirit of God. Talkative people cause divisions and offences in the church and such must be avoided. They serve not our Lord Jesus Christ but their own belly and by good words and fair speeches deceive the hearts of the simple (Romans 16:17-18). Is this you? Go to the Lord in serious prayer to obtain mercy and grace for your salvation and deliverance.

INSTRUCTIONS

- ✓ Pray between 12 midnight to 0400 hrs. This is time to intensify prayer
- ✓ Fast from 12 midnight to 12 midnight (24 hrs.), 1-day prayer & fasting.
- ✓ During the day, also pray

PRAYER POINTS

Take some time to think about how you have been using your tongue. Don't just be quick to pray. Ask the Holy Spirit to minister to you, to reveal things to you that you don't know about your tongue. You may think all is well with your tongue while your tongue is rotten.1 John 1:9–10.

- ☐ I command you the evil spirit of lying, exaggeration, cursing etc. to come to of my mouth, heart and tongue in the mighty name of Jesus Christ
- ☐ Father God, let you fire purge my tongue from contamination of evil communication in the mighty name of Jesus Christ
- ☐ Lord deliver my tongue from becoming a cemetery altar in the mighty name of Jesus Christ
- ☐ I withdraw all the evil words that I have uttered against my life in the mighty name of Jesus Christ
- ☐ I withdraw all the evil words that I have spoken about others in the mighty name of Jesus Christ
- ☐ I withdraw all the evil words that I have spoken against your servants in the mighty name of Jesus Christ
- ☐ I declare and decree that my tongue is wholesome and that with my tongue I shall speak, deliverance, healing, restoration, solutions and life in the mighty name of Jesus Christ
- ☐ I decree that out of my tongue shall flow rivers of life not death in the mighty name of Jesus Christ.

CONFESSION OF FAITH

I brother/sister _____________________________ on this ______day of ________, I was delivered from the spirit of misuse of the tongue and the blood of Jesus Christ bears witness to my deliverance and salvation (1 John 5:8). In the name of the Father, the Son and the Holy Spirit, amen!

ACTION

Don't just pray. If you want to defeat satan and bring shame to him after your deliverance go to the brethren you slandered/hated/gossiped/spread rumours about etc., confess to them "Confess your faults one to another, and pray one for another, that you may be healed. The effectual fervent prayer of a righteous man availeth much "James 5:16. Don't keep it a secret, otherwise, it will be easy for satan to come back and take over your life again and that's why people never experience total and permanent deliverance.

N.B – ask for wisdom from God (James 1:5). Some cases are sensitive so I advise you to seek for counselling from your leader, and also make sure that you spend time in prayer before you act.

TESTIMONY

We overcome satan by the blood of the lamb and by the word of our testimony. Make sure that you testify to the glory of God and to the shame of satan. Pray for your testimony that as you testify it touches others and deliver them. Satan has been using you to fulfil his evil desires now let God use you for the expansion of His kingdom.

DELIVERANCE FROM THE SPIRIT OF BITTERNESS

Hebrews 12:14, 15; Ephesians 4:31-32; 1 Peter 2:23; Luke 23:34; Matthew 6:14-15

Bitterness is like a seed or thought that grows over a period of time. It starts as an attitude and begins to grow in your life. If you have bitterness you have to try and find out how the sin of bitterness got planted in your life. The spirit of bitterness gets planted when you are offended or disappointed by others and dwelling in the hurt will birth failure to forgive. The hurt will germinate in your heart and bitterness will take root. Hebrew 12:14-15; Ephesians 4:31-32; 1 Peter 2:23

Bitterness is something that is painful and often comes upon people as a result of unfair treatment or the perception of been mistreated. Its pillars are unforgiveness and resentment. (1 Peter 2:23).

Bitterness is a root. What is a root? A root is a source, a fountain that is lying under the surface. If you know a plant root system, then it will be easy for you to understand this. Roots do not directly manifest or make themselves known but are a source of nutrition for other parts of the tree. The root's job is not to manifest on the surface but to brew under the surface and nourish the rest of the tree. The same is true with bitterness in a person's soul. It is a hidden element that lies under the surface and out of it springs up negative emotions against others such as anger, irritability, jealousy etc. Are you bitter with somebody somewhere? You are saying that that one I will never forgive. Yes, they hurt you. The fact that you are saying you can't forgive them tells me that you mean you are perfect and you have never hurt anyone anad you will never do it. Stop deceiving yourself. Forgive others. You are not perfect, and no one is perfect but our Father, God (Matthew 6:14-15, Mark 11:25-26, Luke 6:37). I know it might be severely painful. Ask God to help you. Forgiving others and letting go of the pain of bitterness is for your own benefit is not about the offender, if you don't let it go, you are the one who is going to suffer. Go to the Lord in prayer and receive help.

REPENTANCE

Father, I acknowledge that I have held bitterness against ____________________, I confess this as sin and ask you to forgive me.

Thank you for hearing and answering my prayers in Jesus Name, Amen.

INSTRUCTIONS

- ✓ Pray between 12 midnight to 0400 hrs. This is time to intensify prayer
- ✓ Fast from 12 midnight to 12 midnight (24 hrs.), 1-day prayer & fasting.
- ✓ During the day, also pray.

PRAYER POINTS

- ➢ I command the root of bitterness to be uprooted out of my life in the mighty name of Jesus Christ (Hebrews 12:14-15)
- ➢ Father, I forgive all people who ill-treated and mistreated me in the mighty name of Jesus Christ (Ephesians 4:31-32)
- ➢ I get rid of all bitterness, rage, anger, brawling and slander, along with every form of malice in the mighty name of Jesus Christ (Ephesians 4:31-32)

CONFESSION OF FAITH

I brother/sister ____________________ confess that on this ______ day of __________, I was delivered from the spirit and from the root of bitterness and the blood of Jesus Christ bears witness to my deliverance and salvation (1 John 5:8). In the name of the Father, the Son and the Holy Spirit, amen!

ACTION: don't just pray. If you want to defeat satan and bring shame to him, after your deliverance go to the offender, confess to them, tell them that you have been bitter with them because of what they did. Tell them you have forgiven them "Confess your faults one to another, and pray one for another, that you may be healed. The effectual fervent prayer of a righteous man availeth much "James 5:16. Don't keep it a secret, otherwise, it will be easy for satan to come back and take over your life again and that's why people never experience total and permanent deliverance.

N.B - ask for wisdom from God (James 1:5). Some cases are sensitive so I advise you to seek counselling from your leader, and also make sure that you spend time in prayer before you act.

Make sure you are delivered from all other spirits that might have been haunting you, demons work in a team. Example, you might want to forgive your brother/sister and pride/anger says no. It's a sign that some demons are still hanging around. And then to justify yourself will say I am still praying.

ADD MORE ACTION TO YOUR FAITH (James 2:17-18, 20). The person you consider to be the worst offender, the one satan told you never to forgive, pick that person, tell the Holy Spirit you want to do something for that person, therefore, you want Him to lead you. Whatever the Holy Spirit tells you to do it. The Holy Spirit might tell you to buy something for him, or invite him for lunch or pray and fast etc. This will totally uproot bitterness out of your soul and your healing and deliverance will be permanent.

TESTIMONY: We overcome satan by the blood of the lamb and by the word of our testimony. Make sure that you testify to the glory of God and to the shame of satan. Pray for your testimony that as you testify it touches others and deliver them. Satan has been using you to fulfil his evil desires now let God use you for the expansion of His kingdom.

DELIVERANCE FROM THE SPIRIT OF LIMITATION

Mark 11:1-10; Matthew 15:13; Genesis 26:1-14; Acts 28:30-31; Genesis 18:13-14; Isaiah 43:18-19; Jeremiah 32:17-19; Luke 1:37

A limited man is a restricted man who suffers in the midst of plenty. He cannot go beyond the limit the enemy has set for him. He may know what he should attain but still find it difficult to attain it. Limitation makes a man to suffer in the midst of opportunities and possibilities. There is a spirit called the spirit of limitation and until this spirit is dealt with and conquered the victim remains limited in every sphere of life. To suffer limitation in your life means your enemies are in charge and control of your life. They determine how far you can go; they are in charge of your destiny. You may have the potential for greatness, excellence and prosperity but as long as your enemies are in charge, they will set a barrier on your way to greatness.

Satan will introduce things in your life through which he will be able to control your life and keep you in circles. He will make you be careless with money, that is he will use the spirit of mammon to attack you, then you won't pay tithes and if you don't pay tithes there is no how you can prosper. He can use other spirits like laziness, a spirit of waste, procrastination, confusion, discouragement, sicknesses etc.

The devil can also use people to attack you for the purpose of limiting you. In this case, he can use the spirit of accusation, gossip, jealousy, rejection etc.

For you to deal with this spirit and be delivered you should know how satan is using it to attack you. If you don't identify how it is working against your life it can be difficult for you to overcome it because you won't know what you are dealing with. It is, therefore, crucial for you to know how these other spirits operate, then the battle will become easy for you (Hosea 4:6)

INSTRUCTIONS

- ✓ Pray between 12 midnight to 0400 hrs. This is time to intensify prayer
- ✓ Fast and pray for five (5) days
  Day 1: from 12 midnight – 12 noon
  Day 2: from 12 midnight – 12 noon
  Day 3: from 12 midnight – 3 pm
  Day 4: from 12 midnight – 6 pm

Day 5: from 12midnight – 12 midnight
✓ During the day, also pray

PRAYER POINTS

- ☐ I destroy all barriers of limitation, be consumed by Holy Ghost fire in the mighty name of Jesus Christ.
- ☐ I nullify all causes of delay, stagnation and limitation in my life in the mighty name of Jesus Christ.
- ☐ Every seed of limitation planted in my life is uprooted in the mighty name of Jesus Christ.
- ☐ All spiritual cages inhibiting my progress and success break open and release my breakthrough in the mighty name of Jesus Christ.
- ☐ I decree and declare that I am free from the wicked spirit of limitation.

PROPHETIC ACTION - USE THE ANOINTING OIL

Use the anointing oil to anoint yourself as you pray for yourself or for whatever you are praying e.g. your business, tender documents, if it is something academic anoint your books, school reports if its work you can anoint your payslip or your offer letter etc.

Father, God! As I use this anointing oil, I confess with my mouth that no one has an arm like You, Lord, full of power and might (Job 40:9), you have a mighty arm. Your hand is strong, and Your right hand is high (Psalms 89:13). Stretch out Your arm and take away from off my shoulder the burden and from off my neck the yoke (Isaiah 10:27) of limitation in the mighty name of Jesus Christ.

Thank you, Father, for breaking the yoke of limitation into pieces and for scattering all my enemies with your strong arm (Psalms 89:10) in the mighty name of Jesus Christ!

ACTIVATION PRAYER

I decree and declare that from today my (e.g. business) _______________ will prosper and continue to prosper until I am prosperous and that the wealth of the wicked is no longer laying up for me, but it is released now. Those who have been holding on to my wealth be afflicted and be tormented without relief until you release what rightfully belongs to me. I command satan to cough it up, spit it out, lose it, release it, vomit it and let it come to me in the mighty name of Jesus Christ. (Genesis 26:13;Psalms 66:12;Ecclesiastes 2:26;Job 20:15-18).

CONFESSION OF FAITH

I brother/sister____________ declare that, on this ______day of ____________, the burden and the yoke of limitation was taken away from off my shoulder and neck and was destroyed by the anointing of the Holy Spirit (Isaiah 10:27) and the blood of Jesus Christ bears witness to my deliverance and salvation (1 John 5:8). In the name of the Father, the Son and the Holy Spirit, amen!

ACTION: Don't just pray, add action to your prayers. You have been limited, now you are trusting God for a breakthrough. It may be your business, your plan to marry, career, finance etc. Take a seed, by faith go and sow into the grace and anointing of your man of God. The man of God will pray for you and release uncommon favour, financial grace, favour for academic excellence, it will depend on what you want. Don't waste time act quickly. If you are still struggling with the spirit of mammon, selfishness, stinginess this will be difficult for you. Remember demons work in clusters.

TESTIMONY: We overcome satan by the blood of the lamb and by the word of our testimony. When God opens doors for you and gives you breakthrough make sure that you testify to the glory of His name and to the shame of satan. Pray for your testimony that as you testify it touches others and deliver them. Satan has been using you to fulfil his evil desires now let God use you for the expansion of His kingdom.

DELIVERANCE FROM THE ACCUSING SPIRIT

The accusing spirit is an anti-Christ spirit because it approaches people with no love but as a voice of condemnation. It works through the voice of condemnation. It constantly tells you how bad you are, how useless you are, how sinful you are, how much of failure you are. It tears up rather than build up. It's a Pharisenism spirit (Matthew 23:4; 2 Corinthians 3:6).

This spirit attacks by bringing up your past failures and mistakes. This spirit can also cause people to create stories which are not true about you to attack you. It works or operates by laying burdens on people (Galatians 5:4). The accusing spirit is a voice. It speaks to its victim directly to bring them under condemnation (2 Corinthians 11:13-15).

The devil is called the accuser of our brethren (Revelation 12:10). He is an accuser. He came to God in Job 1:9, 11 and accused Job of being an evil man. Satan wants to destroy your testimony and one of the things he will do is to accuse you. He will give people a wrong picture of who you are to stop you, embarrass you and bring shame into your life, to make people give up on you. The devil can go around telling people at work, in your neighbourhood, at school even in the church that you are a thief and when people hear that they lose trust in you, he can tell people that you are a drunkard while you are not. All these he does with the ultimate purpose of destroying your testimony and to bring shame in your life.

If you have the experience of people saying you are this and that, you have done this, you were seen there doing that, you are in a relationship with so and so while you have done none of those things just know the accuser is after your testimony. If satan can manage to tint your testimony you become vulnerable to his attacks.

When satan attacks you resist him, stand upon the word of God and hold on unto your testimony. He accused Job to the point of making him suffer terribly but Job held on unto the Lord, and when he forgave his friends the Lord turned his situation around for good.

People might have said a lot of things about you.

Don't give up. Your deliverance now does not matter the damage, the shame and embarrassment satan might have brought into your life. You will be delivered, not only that but the Lord will restore to you everything that you lost. God healed Job and restored all that he lost.

FRUITS OF THE ACCUSING SPIRIT

    ☐ Self-hate

- ☐ Guilt (Adam & Eve)
- ☐ Shame (Adam & Eve)
- ☐ Fear
- ☐ Doubt
- ☐ Unbelief
- ☐ Hate
- ☐ Judge mentalism
- ☐ Critical spirit
- ☐ Resentment
- ☐ Feelings of hopelessness

THE ACCUSING SPIRIT'S MISSION

John 10:10 its mission is to steal your peace, to destroy your testimony, to tear you apart, destroy your faith, to wear you down spiritually. It wants you to walk in guilt.

The accusing spirit is a blaming spirit that speculates in digging up the past and creating stories. This spirit works hand in hand with a critical spirit or judgementalism.

HOW TO DEAL WITH THE SPIRIT OF ACCUSATION (HOW TO BE DELIVERED)

(2 Corinthians 10:5) Cast it down. Renew your mind with God's word; this will help you to undo the damage that might have been done to your thinking pattern.

1. **REPENT**- when you heard that people are talking evil about you how did you respond? Did you respond to the Jesus Christ way? That is out of godly love. The word of God teaches us that we should bless our persecutors and when we do that we shall be blessed (Mathew 5:11). Maybe when you heard all that people were saying about you, you allowed the devil to use you also. You started foaming, threatening and swearing, by so doing you grieved the Holy Spirit of God, if that is your case repent. Some people when they hear that others are talking about them in retaliation and revenge they speak evil against the offender, but now if you behave like that what is the difference between you and satan. You are the light of the world (Mathew 5:14, 16). The more darkness

attacks you, the more your light must shine.

2. **FORGIVE**- forgive all the people whom satan has used to make you suffer accusations. Remember if you don't forgive you can't be forgiven (Mathew 5:23-24; 6:12-15)

3. **ASK GOD TO HEAL AND RESTORE YOU** – the spirit of accusation wants to leave you wounded and bleeding, where possible it destroys completely (John 10:10). Once you become a victim of this demon your life will be like Job's.

4. **COMMAND THE SPIRIT TO COME OUT OF YOUR LIFE** – you have the power in the name of Jesus Christ. Use that power to compel and expel satan out of your life (Luke 10; 19).

5. **BELIEVE THAT YOU ARE FREE** – after you have prayed, believe with all your heart that you are free and that you have received a restoration of all things.

6. **PRAISE GOD FOR DELIVERING YOU** – finish your prayer by returning the glory to God.

INSTRUCTIONS

- ✓ Pray between 12 midnight to 0400 hrs. This is time to intensify prayer
- ✓ Fast and pray for three (3) days
  Day 1: from 12 midnight – 3 pm
  Day 2: from 12 midnight – 6 pm
  Day 3: from 12midnight – 12 midnight
- ✓ During the day, also pray

PRAYER POINTS

- ➢ I release the voice of the blood of Jesus Christ against every satanic voice of accusation and condemnation that are speaking against my life, family, business, career, finances, ministry etc. in the realm of the spirit (Hebrews 12:24)
- ➢ You altar of accusation erected by satan to attack my ministry/ service unto the Lord (Mathew 12:10) through the blood of Jesus Christ, receive thunder and die
- ➢ I command all my accusers to disappear and never to appear again in the mighty name of Jesus (John 8:10)

- ➤ You satan the devil, the accuser of the brethren, I rebuke you and cast you out from my life in Jesus mighty name (Revelation 12:10)
- ➤ You satan the devil, I declare and announce in the realm of the spirit that the confidence that you had, that you have destroyed my ministry, family, business etc. is uprooted and destroyed (Job 18:14) in Jesus mighty name.

PROPHETIC ACTION – USE THE HOLY COMMUNION

Father God, of my Lord Jesus Christ, I thank you for the body of your Son, Jesus Christ that was broken for me and His blood that was shed for my sins. As I eat the body of Jesus and drink His blood (John 6:54), I decree and declare that I am delivered from the accusing spirit, and my mind and thoughts are covered by the blood of Jesus Christ (Exodus 12:13) and I am made perfect through His blood of the covenant (Hebrews 13:20 -21) and my conscience is purged from dead works to serve the living God through the blood of Jesus (Hebrews 9:14). Spirit of accusation I have overcome you through the blood of Jesus Christ (Revelation 12:11) and I receive the benefits of the new covenant through the blood of Jesus Christ (Mathew 26:28).

CONFESSION OF FAITH

I decree and declare that I brother/sister _____________on this ______ day of ____________my life, business, family, ministry etc. was sprinkled and purified by the blood of Jesus Christ my Lord and personal saviour from evil works of the accusing spirit (Hebrews 10:17) and the blood of Jesus Christ bears witness to my deliverance and salvation (1 John 5:8).In Jesus mighty name …. amen!

TESTIMONY: We overcome satan by the blood of the lamb and by the word of our testimony. When God fights for you and defeats your accusers for you make sure that you testify to the glory of His name and to the shame of satan. Pray for your testimony that as you testify it touches others and deliver them. Satan has been using you to fulfil his evil desires now let God use for the expansion of His kingdom.

DELIVERANCE FROM THE SPIRIT OF GRIEF

Grief is a natural response to pain. There is nothing wrong with grieving.The time of grieving serves the purpose of deliverance. When you lose someone or something that you loved dearly or when plans don't happen the way you expected, or when life does not give you what you were waiting for and it seems like dreams are shattered and hope is lost you will definitely feel pain. You will feel like God let me die now. My spouse is dead, I have failed form five, I have lost my job, let me die. (Eccl 7:3; Psalms 30:5; 56:8; 46:10; 91:1-2). Grieving should be for a moment. Godly grieving is a medicine, it brings deliverance. When you are grieving, don't grief like a sinner? God does not forbid us to grieve or mourn the death of a loved one. When you are grieving you are dealing with the very real pain of loss.

Jesus our Lord and saviour, when He saw Mary and Martha in anguish for the death of their brother Lazarus, He wept and groaned. Jesus Christ felt and expressed human sorrow. Healing a broken heart is a process, don't rush it. Don't pretend that all is well when you know you are grieving. A grief that is not dealt with or left unresolved may trigger depression, thoughts of suicide, high blood pressure or other serious problems that will put your life into more danger.

Satan comes to steal, to kill and to destroy (John 10:10). Through grief, he steals your joy and peace. Once he takes away your joy it means he has taken over your life. He will then do whatever he wants to do with your life. When you don't have the joy of the Lord and the joy of your salvation it means you have no strength because the joy of the Lord is your strength (Psalms 147:3). Any situation that you find yourself in is not experienced by you alone but it is a common experience to all of us. Satan wants to tell you and make you feel like your situation is unique. If he can succeed in telling you that and you believe his lies you will automatically reject every help, regardless of how others attempt to help you because in your mind you will be saying, they don't know what it means to lose a spouse, a child, job, they don't know the pain I am feeling, they don't know what I am going through, they can't feel what I am feeling.

Ecclesiastes 3:14, to everything there is a season, a time for everything under heaven, a time to weep and a time to laugh, a time to mourn, and a time to dance.

The spirit of grief can enter your life through things that happen in and around your life such as;

- ☐ A broken relationship
- ☐ The death of a loved one
- ☐ A series of disappointments
- ☐ Events that happened to you breaking your heart repeatedly
- ☐ Damaging and traumatic life events like being raped or sexually abuse, divorce etc.
- ☐ Repeated attacks from satan like losing your job, family members dying one after the other

What are you grieving?

It can be; the death of your spouse, maybe your spouse left you, the death of a loved one, loss of a job, academic failure, family problems, financial losses, the negative report about your health etc.

Symptoms of grief - Grief can affect your thinking, behaviour, emotions, relationships, character, Christianity and health.

Physical - Crying, headaches, loss of appetite, difficulty in sleeping, feelings of heaviness, fatigue, pains

Emotional - Sadness, feelings of worry, anger, frustration, easily irritated, loneliness, resentment.

Spiritual - Angry at God, questioning God, loss of appetite for spiritual things, just going to church for the sake of going, not interested in telling others about Christ, feelings of backsliding, satanic dreams, blaming other Christians, blaming God, not growing spiritually, disobedience to God's word.

How to be delivered

1. Be born again

If you realise that the way you are grieving is not normal or should I say is not godly, then know you have backslidden or maybe you were never born again. There is a way a child of God grieves. Marry and Martha grieved but in their grieving, they put their trust in Christ "if you were here our brother would not have died (John 11:21-23) "Jesus also grieved for Lazarus (verse 35), but He also put His trust in God "father thank you, that you have heard me (verses 41 – 43). When your grieving becomes a disgrace to God just know you are not a Christian. Don't behave like you are the first person to lose a spouse, job, child etc. The situation you are going through, you are not the only one experiencing it, many have gone through it and many are still going through it but they never left God, they did not stop going to church or whatsoever (1 Corinthians 10:13).In Luke 2:36 – 38, we read about prophetess Anna. She lived only for seven years with her husband and she became a widow and for about 84 years she was a widow. Anna did not backslide, she departed not from the temple, and she served God with fasting and prayers night and day. The problem here is not that you lost somebody or something. The problem is, you are not born again, and that's why you can't be comforted. Give your life to Jesus, be born again and you will be delivered from the demon of grief.

2. Take comfort in knowing that Jesus has borne our grieves and carried our sorrows

Jesus carried all our pains, including loss, rejection, and betrayal and death. What is it that you are going through that Jesus did not experience (Isaiah 53:1 – 10)? Allow Jesus to lead you through the valley of the shadow of death (Psalms 23:4)

Maybe you have been grieving the death of someone you loved so much. I don't know who that person is. The last enemy to be defeated is death (1 Corinthian15:26). When a person dies, sometimes you hear people saying God has taken him or her. Death is an enemy, there is an angel called the angel of death. This angel of death comes to take our loved one away from us but Jesus takes them away from death, He takes them away from the pain and sufferings of death. Sickness is a pain of death, it is a bullet that death releases to torture and torment people. When a person dies, God has taken him or her from the pain and torture of death. When one is sick, they are under the attack of the Altar of Death.

If you have been grieving the death of a loved one, don't be angry at God. Thank God that He delivered your beloved from the pain of death. That's why Apostle Paul said we should not grieve like those who have no hope (1 Thessalonians 4:13-18). The death of a sinner is different from the death of a Christian and that's why the Bible says God has no pleasure in the death of a sinner (Ezekiel 33:11). Be comforted with the words of Apostle Paul "for to me to live is Christ and to die is gain – Philippians 1:21) and be delivered from grief.

3. Seek counselling

Without counsel purposes are disappointed, but in the multitude of counsellors, they are established (Proverbs 15:22). Don't die a silent death. Go to your man of God for counselling. You are the one who is suffering. Admit that you need help and you shall be helped. Jesus does not want to see you suffering, He wants to comfort you and give you peace "and the peace of God, which passeth all understanding, shall keep your hearts and minds through Christ Jesus – Philippians 4:7" for the chastisement of our peace was upon Him and with His stripes, we are healed – Isaiah 53:5). Jesus Loves you, He is calling you "Come unto me, all ye that labour and are heavily laden, and I will give you rest Mathew 11:28). It does not matter what you are grieving and for how long you have been grieving, surrender all unto Jesus "casting all your care upon Him for He careth for you – 1 Peter 5:7".

4. Admit that you need deliverance and healing

Identify what you are grieving and its cause. Dedicate yourself to making it change. Change does not happen by chance; your effort will be needed for deliverance to happen. Make a plan as to how you are going to make it happen.

5. Let go of the past

For you to be delivered you must let the past go. Do not let your past bind you, blind and haunt you. Isaiah 43:18-19, God wants to do a new thing in your life. Letting go of the past means facing reality. You hear somebody saying I don't care even if you can die when that person dies reality has come.

Sometimes it may not be that you are an ''I don't care "it maybe you never thought that a thing like that could happen. When it finally happens, you are facing reality. So letting go of your past can include coping with the death of a loved one, loss of a job, academic failure, relationship break up, divorce etc. Letting the past go may be the hardest thing you will ever do. For example, if it's a case of divorce, even if that man used to abuse you and your marriage was full of troubles and problems, you may still struggle to let go of the hurting experiences, but you have to let it go.

- First of all, start with yourself. Identify areas of your life where you need to forgive yourself. Be at peace with yourself. Admit your mistakes. Face your shame and guilt, deal with your mistakes.
- Secondly, seek forgiveness from those whom you have wronged. Where you are wrong admit that you are wrong. Do not harden your heart. Apologise and ask for forgiveness if you need to.
- Thirdly, forgive those who wronged you, Ephesians 4:31, get rid of bitterness and anger. Your feelings affect you, not the other person. Resentment does not change your past; it does not resolve your problems but rather make them worse (Job 5:2). Just as God forgave you, your sins, forgive others. If you do not forgive, God cannot forgive you.
- Accept that in life there are things that happen and you can't change them. You should stop allowing your past mistakes and failures to manipulate you. Forget what is behind. You must let the past go in order to get on with the future. Learn from your past but do not let your past control you. Do not allow satan to paralyze you with memories of the past.
- Talk to the people involved
- Allow God to cleanse your memories
- Let go of the emotions and feelings of your past
- Letting go of your past also is about burying your pride
- Take care of your thinking pattern.be aware of your thoughts
- Ask God to connect you to people who can help you. New connections, divine connections.

PRAYER

- [ ] If you are not born again or you have backslidden, repent, give your life to Jesus Christ and be born again.
- [ ] Pray for your offenders. Forgive them and pray for their salvation. Ask God to forgive them.
- [ ] Ask God to deliver you from grieving.
- [ ] Conduct self-deliverance.

CHAPTER 3
DELIVERANCE FROM THE SPIRIT OF STAGNATION

Stagnation means remaining on the same spot or position without any reasonable progress despite available opportunities or resources (Deuteronomy 1:3-6; Acts 3:1-10). satan will set roadblocks and barriers to hinder you to progress in life. God wants you to flourish and make progress in every area of your life (Jeremiah 17:17-18). Acts 3:1-10, the man at the gate called beautiful was crippled, he could not do anything for himself. He became a beggar. Isaiah 60:2, shows you are to rise and shine. The man at the beautiful gate was like a star that could not shine. He was stagnant and stuck.

When your life is crippled you can have the potential for greatness but still remain in one place. When you are held hostage by the spirit of stagnation you are like a person who is stuck in a traffic jam, such a one cannot reach his destination at the desired time. And this is what stagnation will do to you. When you are stuck you cannot do the things that you want to do when you want to. In traffic, jam one may try to hoot, shout, overtake or even change lanes but all this can't work, he is stuck. The same thing applies to you, when you are under the garment of stagnation, you can try to fast, pray, have night prayers but until you tear the garment apart and go free nothing changes. Stagnation means there is no movement, no progress at all. it means progress and growth has stopped.

Identify areas of your life where progress and growth have stopped. Confront the spirit aggressively. Command it out of your life, family, business, ministry etc.

INSTRUCTIONS

- ✓ Pray between 12 midnight to 0400 hrs. This is time to intensify prayer
- ✓ Fast and pray for five (5) days
  Day 1: from 12 midnight – 12 noon

Day 2: from 12 midnight – 12 noon
Day 3: from 12 midnight – 3 pm
Day 4: from 12 midnight – 6 pm
Day 5: from 12midnight – 12 midnight
✓ During the day, also pray.

PRAYER POINTS

- ➤ I decree and declare that the breaker, my Lord Jesus Christ is gone up before me and broken through every spirit of stagnation and my life is free from stagnation – Micah 2:13
- ➤ I nullify and destroy all causes of stagnation in my life and I declare that I flourish like a palm tree and grow like a cedar in Lebanon – Psalms 92:12
- ➤ I pull down strongholds of stagnation and I declare that my latter end shall greatly increase – Job 8:7
- ➤ I command that every seed of stagnation planted in my life, family, business, career, ministry etc. be uprooted in the name of Jesus – Jeremiah 1:10
- ➤ I command every evil tree planted in my family, business, ministry etc. to be uprooted and be planted into the sea – Luke 17:6.

PROPHETIC ACT - USE THE ANOINTING OIL

Father, God! as I use this anointing oil, I destroy all ungodly covenants, oaths and pledges that I have made with my mouth and I destroy all ungodly covenants made by my ancestors to idols and demons (Mathew 5:33; Exodus 23:32) that have brought me under the garment of stagnation, be destroyed in the mighty name of Jesus Christ. Your garment of stagnation, I command arrows of the Lord to come upon you like lightning and destroy you in the mighty name of Jesus Christ (Zechariah 9:14).

ACTIVATION PRAYER

I decree and declare that the garment of stagnation that was holding my life is destroyed, the Lord God almighty has gone ahead of me and He has made the crooked places straight. He has broken in pieces the gates of brass and cut asunder the bars of iron, He has granted unto me riches in glory in Christ Jesus and hidden riches of secret

places. I declare that from now onwards my life is like a watered garden and I shall be called blessed in the mighty name Jesus Christ. (Isaiah 45:1-3; 60:10-17; Philippian 4:19).

CONFESSION OF FAITH

I brother/sister _____________declare that on this _________ day of _______ the evil spirit of stagnation was uprooted out of my life and the blood of Jesus Christ bears witness to my salvation and deliverance in the name of the father, the Son and the Holy Spirit.

ACTION: After praying and fasting go to your man of God for confirmation of your deliverance, sow a seed as the Spirit of God leads you (Romans 8:14). You can sow a seed for your ministry, children, business, financial breakthrough, marriage etc.

Remember the word of the Lord says 'believe in the Lord your God and you shall be established and believe in the prophets-His servants and you shall prosper (2 Chronicles 20:20).

TESTIMONY: We overcome satan by the blood of the lamb and by the word of our testimony. When God opens doors for you and gives you breakthrough make sure that you testify to the glory of His name and to the shame of satan. Pray for your testimony that as you testify it touches others and deliver them. Satan has been using you to fulfil his evil desires now let God use you for the expansion of His kingdom.

DELIVERANCE FROM THE SPIRIT OF EMOTIONAL WOUNDS

If you get involved with people, you are going to get hurt. Emotional hurts and wounds hinder your faith (Psalms 34:19). Maybe you are wounded and bleeding emotionally, I don't know what might have caused you all that pain. Hear this; the Lord will deliver you. Only believe. Maybe as you are reading now, you feel alone, abandoned, scared and weak, you feel like your situation is hard, wrenching and painful. Whatever situation the enemy is using in your past to haunt you and cause you to feel forgotten, guilty, bad and ashamed, let me tell you, you are about to smile because "the righteous person may have many troubles but the LORD delivers him from them all".

Maybe the people you trusted or someone you trust, including your own family, a friend(s) or your spouse hurt and treat you in the worst way, hold on unto Jesus Christ.

HOW WILL YOU KNOW YOU NEED EMOTIONAL HEALING?

- ☐ Irritability-you easily gets irritable with others even if they are not doing anything wrong.
- ☐ Bad feelings –feelings of anger, hate, resentment etc. seem to rise up within you at the slightest offence from others.
- ☐ Hard to forgive others
- ☐ Hard to feel loved
- ☐ Self-hate
- ☐ Easily frustrated
- ☐ Retaliation urges
- ☐ Perfectionism
- ☐ Feelings of hopelessness

If you want to be healed the key thing is forgiveness. Forgive those who have wronged you. Ask God to help you by His grace, He will help you and it will be easy for you to forgive. If you harbour wrong feelings in your heart about other people you can't be delivered. It is important also to know how you got wounded so that you may know exactly what you are dealing with.

INSTRUCTIONS

- ✓ Pray between 12 midnight to 0400 hrs. This is time to intensify prayer
- ✓ Fast and pray for three (3) days
  Day 1: from 12 midnight – 3 pm
  Day 2: from 12 midnight – 6 pm
  Day 3: from 12midnight – 12 midnight
- ✓ During the day, also pray

PRAYER POINTS

- ☐ Father, God! I forgive all people who hurt and wounded me in the past, even the one I was finding it difficult to forgive in the mighty name of Jesus Christ.

- ☐ Father, I ask you to remove the shame and guilt of my past experiences from my life in the mighty name of Jesus Christ.
- ☐ Heal me Lord and I shall be healed in the mighty name of Jesus Christ.
- ☐ Jesus Christ my Lord, I open up my emotional wounds to you for cleansing and healing, heal me.
- ☐ You satan of emotional wounds, I decree and declare that you have no power over my life, I am delivered, I am healed and sanctified in the mighty name of Jesus Christ.

ACTIVATION PRAYER

I decree and declare that by the stripes of the Lord Jesus, I am delivered and healed from emotional wounds for He was wounded for my transgressions, He was bruised for my iniquities, the chastisement of my peace was upon Him; and with His stripes, I am healed, I put a halt to all distractive, disturbing and destructive measures, for, for this reason, was the Son of God made manifest, that He would destroy the works of the devil (1 John 3:8; Isaiah 53:5) in the mighty name of Jesus Christ.

CONFESSION OF FAITH

I brother/sister _______________ confess that, on this ______ day of __________, I was delivered and healed from emotional wounds and the blood of Jesus Christ bears witness to my deliverance and salvation (1 John 5:8). In the name of the Father, the Son and the Holy Spirit, amen!

ACTION: Don't just pray. If you want to defeat satan and bring shame to him, after your deliverance go to the offender, confess to them, tell them that you have been bitter with them because of what they did. Tell them you have forgiven them "Confess your faults one to another, and pray one for another, that you may be healed. The effectual fervent prayer of a righteous man availeth much "James 5:16. Don't keep it a secret, otherwise, it will be easy for satan to come back and take over your life again and that's why people never experience total and permanent deliverance.

N.B:- ask for wisdom from God (James 1:5). Some cases are sensitive so I advise you to seek counselling from your leader, and also make sure that you spend time in prayer before you act.

Make sure you are delivered from all other spirits that might have been haunting you. Demons work in a team. Example, you might want to forgive your brother/sister and pride/anger says no. It is a sign that some demons are still hanging around. And then to justify yourself, you will say I am still praying.

ADD MORE ACTION TO YOUR FAITH (James 2:17-18, 20). The person you consider to be the worst offender, the one satan told you never to forgive, pick that person, tell the Holy Spirit you want to do something for that person, therefore, you want Him to lead you. Whatever the Holy Spirit tells you to do it. The Holy Spirit might tell you to buy something for him, or invite him for lunch or pray and fast etc. This will totally uproot bitterness out of your soul and your healing and deliverance will be permanent.

TESTIMONY: We overcome satan by the blood of the lamb and by the word of our testimony. Make sure that you testify to the glory of God and to the shame of satan. Pray for your testimony that as you testify it touches others and deliver them. Satan has been using you to fulfil his evil desires now let God use for the expansion of His kingdom.

DELIVERANCE FROM BAD HABITS

Many people struggle with bad habits and wish they could stop (John 10:10, 1 Corinthians 10:13). Anything you do without consciously thinking about it, or without demanding to do it, it is a habit.

To banish a bad habit, you must understand things about yourself and the habit. Each habit gives us a perceived benefit. Now, you must know what habit you want to get rid of. How is the habit affecting your life? What has this habit replaced in your life? What do you benefit from the habit? Decide to stop, never to do it again, see change occur.

To get rid of negative habits that stop you from achieving your goals and your highest potential

1. Write down the bad habit that you want to get rid of.

2. Meditate on the power of God.

3. Pray, depend upon the grace and power of God.

4. See yourself free.

5. Praise and thank God.

INSTRUCTIONS

- ✓ Pray between 12 midnight to 0400 hrs. This is time to intensify prayer
- ✓ Fast and pray for seven (7) days
  Day 1: from 12 midnight – 12 noon
  Day 2: from 12 midnight – 12 noon
  Day 3: from 12 midnight – 3 pm
  Day 4: from 12 midnight – 5 pm
  Day 5: from 12 midnight – 7 pm
  Day 6: from 12 midnight – 7 pm
  Day 7: from 12 midnight – 7 pm
- ✓ During the day, also pray

PRAYER POINTS

- ☐ I have completely lost any desire for (e.g. masturbation) ______________________________ and I command it to come out of my appetite in the mighty name of Jesus Christ
- ☐ I bind all spirits of this addiction and I command them to come out of my life in Jesus mighty name
- ☐ I command all spirits of guilt, shame, setback, failure and condemnation that came upon my life as a result of this bad habit to come out of my life in Jesus mighty name.
- ☐ You power of addiction you are bound and you will have no hold on me any more in Jesus Name
- ☐ You satanic chain that has been binding me you are destroyed, be gone from me and never return to me in Jesus mighty name.

CONFESSION OF FAITH

I brother/sister ____________ declare that on this ______ day of ________, I was delivered from the bad habit of ________________ am delivered now and the blood of Jesus Christ bears witness to my deliverance and salvation (1 John 5:8). In Jesus Mighty Name. Amen!

ACTION

After being delivered from a bad habit, make sure you replace it with another good one. If you were delivered from watching movies, use that time for something beneficial, like doing school work, going out to evangelise, reading Bible etc.

''Altar destroys Altar – Habit destroys Habit, Altar versus Altar – Habit versus Habit''

TESTIMONY: We overcome satan by the blood of the lamb and by the word of our testimony. Make sure that you testify to the glory of God and to the shame of satan. Pray for your testimony that as you testify it touches others and deliver them. Satan has been using you to fulfil his evil desires now let God use you for the expansion of His kingdom.

DELIVERANCE FROM THE SPIRIT OF UNFORGIVENESS

Romans 12:17; 19-21; Matthew 18:21-22; Colossians 3:13; John 15:12

Are you harbouring unforgiveness in your heart? Could there be someone that hurt you in whatever way that you are failing to forgive? Do not repay anyone evil for evil, do not take revenge but leave room for God's wrath. If your enemy is hungry feed him, if he is thirsty, give him something to drink (Romans 12:17; 19-21). Remember, if you don't forgive God can't forgive you.

(Luke 6:37; Mark 11:25), if you do not forgive it;

- shows you don't really love Jesus
- Prevents God from forgiving your sins (Matthew 6:15).
- Opens your life to satan (Matthew 18:23-35).
- Hinders your prayers to be answered (Mark 11:24-25).
- Defiles a person (Hebrews 12:15).
- Prevents you from being fruitful spiritually (John 15:5).

INSTRUCTIONS

- ✓ Pray between 12 midnight to 0400 hrs. This is time to intensify prayer
- ✓ Fast from 12 midnight to 12 midnight (24 hrs.), 1-day prayer & fasting.
- ✓ During the day, also pray.

PRAYER POINTS

- ☐ Father God! I confess that in the past I held unforgiveness and bitterness in my heart against people who hurt or disappointed me, now I recognise this as sin and ask you to forgive me.
- ☐ I now freely forgive them and ask you to bless them.
- ☐ Thank you, Father, for freedom from a load of unforgiveness and bitterness.
- ☐ I destroy all curses that entered my life because of unforgiveness, be destroyed in the mighty name of Jesus Christ.
- ☐ I decree and declare that I am free from forgiveness.

CONFESSION FAITH

I brother/sister ___________________ declare that on this ______ day of ___________, I was delivered from unforgiveness of ______________ am delivered now and the blood of Jesus Christ bears witness to my deliverance and salvation (1 John 5:8). In Jesus Mighty Name. Amen!

ACTION: Don't just pray. If you want to defeat satan and bring shame to him, after your deliverance go to the offender, confess to them, tell them that you have been harbouring unforgiveness in your heart against them because of what they did. Tell them you have forgiven them "Confess your faults one to another, and pray one for another, that you may be healed. The effectual fervent prayer of a righteous man availeth much "James 5:16. Don't keep it a secret, otherwise, it will be easy for satan to come back and take over your life again and that's why people never experience total and permanent deliverance.

N.B: make sure you are delivered from all other spirits that might have been haunting you. demons work as a team. Example, you might want to forgive your brother/sister and pride/anger says no. It is a sign that some demons are still hanging around. And then to justify yourself, you will say am still praying.

ADD MORE ACTION TO YOUR FAITH (James 2:17-18, 20). The person you consider to be the worst offender, the one satan told you never to forgive, pick that person, tell the Holy Spirit you want to do something for that person, therefore, you want Him to lead you. Whatever the Holy Spirit tells you, do it. The Holy Spirit might tell you to buy something for him, or invite him for lunch or pray and fast etc. This will totally uproot bitterness out of your soul and your healing and deliverance will be permanent.

TESTIMONY: We overcome satan by the blood of the lamb and by the word of our testimony. Make sure that you testify to the glory of God and to the shame of satan. Pray for your testimony that as you testify it touches others and deliver them. Satan has been using you to fulfil his evil desires now let God use you for the expansion of His kingdom.

DELIVERANCE FROM THE SPIRIT OF SUSPICION

Proverbs 1:5

Saul was suspicious of David, and he imagined all kinds of things about him. Suspicion becomes a stronghold in our lives when we refuse to put God first, to give our lives to Him and allow the Holy Spirit to guide us. Suspicion prevents us from seeing the good light, the blessing and the potential.

To be suspicious is to have a feeling or a thought that something is likely or probably true. It is the positive tendency to doubt the trustworthiness of appearances and therefore to believe that one has detected possibilities of something unreliable or the like.

(1 Corinthians 13:7) 'Love bears all things, believes all things, and hopes all things'. Remember love covers a multitude of sins. When you love your brother you won't be unduly suspicious about them. Love hopes for the best from others, not negative things. Suspicion

will make your relationship with other people harder. Let me tell you why you are always suspicious of others. Do you want to know?

1. It is because you don't have God's love.
2. It is because you are a hypocrite and now you think everybody else is like you and now you judge others by your motives and character.

It might be that you are possessed.

When you see a brother with a lady you don't know, you come to conclusions that the brother has backslidden. Is it not you who has backslidden? When you see brethren standing together, you conclude that they are gossiping. You know why because you are a gossiper. Why are you always spying others? It is because you are not faithful. A true child of God has the spirit of discernment not the spirit of suspicion. Christians discern, they don't suspect. If a brother has a fiancée and does not trust her, he will always want to police her cell phone. Spirit of suspicion is a relationship destroyer. It is a wrong seed of mistrust. When you are drunk with this spirit, when you look at others you see liars, pretenders, hypocrites and so forth.

HOW TO AVOID SUSPICION

- Be ready to see the good in others than the bad (1 Corinthians 13:7).
- Follow God's law, allow the fruit of the spirit to live within you (Ephesians 5:9-12).
- Never give in to an occasion of sin or lawlessness (2 Timothy 2:15).
- Forgive each other. Resolve any problem and warn fellow believers before suspicion takes over (James 4:11).

INSTRUCTIONS

- ✓ Pray between 12 midnight to 0400 hrs. This is time to intensify prayer
- ✓ Fast from 12 midnight to 12 midnight (24 hrs.), 1-day prayer & fasting.
- ✓ During the day, also pray

PRAYER POINTS

- ☐ Father forgive me for allowing satan to use me, I admit that I allowed the spirit of suspicion to rule my life and because of this spirit I have hurt others. Forgive me please Lord, in the mighty name of Jesus Christ.
- ☐ I pray for all people that I have hurt and wronged, I ask you, Father, heal them and help them by your grace to forgive me.
- ☐ You spirit of suspicion, I command you come out of my thoughts and emotions, be gone in the mighty name of Jesus Christ.
- ☐ I open my spirit to the Spirit of God and I receive the gift of discernment in Jesus mighty name.
- ☐ I decree and declare that I am free from the spirit of suspicion in the mighty name of Jesus Christ.

CONFESSION OF FAITH

I brother/sister _________________ declare that on this _____ day of _____________, I was delivered from the spirit of suspicion __________ am delivered now and the blood of Jesus Christ bears witness to my deliverance and salvation (1 John 5:8). In Jesus Mighty Name. Amen!

TESTIMONY: We overcome satan by the blood of the lamb and by the word of our testimony. Make sure that you testify to the glory of God and to the shame of satan. Pray for your testimony that as you testify it touches others and deliver them. Satan has been using you to fulfil his evil desires now let God use you for the expansion of His kingdom.

DELIVERANCE FROM THE SPIRIT OF CRITICISM

Criticism is an act of judging as a critique; to find fault, to blame or to condemn (Romans 14:10-13).

WHAT IS A CRITICAL SPIRIT?

It is an obsessive attitude, a fault-finding spirit which seeks to tear down others rather than build them; it destroys people. Do you have a critical spirit? It is dangerous to have a critical or judgemental spirit because instead of being a blessing to others you are going to be a stumbling block to them and hence destroy their faith. A critical spirit is a poisonous character that is if one has this spirit they are poisonous. If this spirit is not confronted it will cause a lot of damage to the church. This spirit does not build but rather it destroys.

CHARACTERISTICS OF DESTRUCTIVE CRITICISM

- It dwells on the negative. People with this spirit are constantly complaining and are usually upset with somebody or something.
- They have little control over their tongue, their temper, tendencies for gossip, slander, strife and malice (Romans 1:29-32).
- It can be very detrimental and damaging to a person's faith or the health and vitality of the ministry.
- A critical person expects and hopes that everything will have something wrong in it.
- Critical people hurt themselves and others as well.

WHAT CAUSES A CRITICAL SPIRIT?

1. Our sinful or selfish nature.

2. Poor self-concept

3. Little or no grace

4. negativity- a negative emotional focus on bad attitude

5. Insecurity

6. Immaturity

7. Un-renewed mind (Romans 12:2).

8. A root of bitterness (Hebrews 12:15).

9. Bad company (1 Corinthians 15:33)

10. The devil (Ephesians 4:7; Revelations 12:10).

11. Self-accusation

12. Comparison / Competition

INSTRUCTIONS

- ✓ Pray between 12 midnight to 0400 hrs. This is time to intensify prayer
- ✓ Fast from 12 midnight to 12 midnight (24 hrs.), 1-day prayer & fasting.
- ✓ During the day, also pray

PRAYER POINTS

- ☐ Father forgive me for having been a critical person. I know I have harmed myself and hurt your people as a result of the spirit of criticism
- ☐ I command all spirits of; hurt, rejection, fear, anger, wrath, sadness, depression, discouragement, grief, bitterness and unforgiveness to come out of my emotions in the mighty name of Jesus Christ
- ☐ You spirit of criticism; I uproot you by your roots come out of my emotions in the mighty name of Jesus Christ.
- ☐ I soak my emotions in the blood of Jesus Christ for cleansing in the mighty name of Jesus Christ.
- ☐ I soak my emotions in the fire of the Holy Ghost for purging and refining in the mighty name of Jesus Christ.
- ☐ I command you spirit to come out of my spiritual appetite in the mighty name of Jesus Christ.
- ☐ I decree and declare that I am delivered from you spirit of criticism in the mighty name of Jesus Christ.

CONFESSION OF FAITH

I brother/sister _________________ declare that on this _____ day of __________, I was delivered from the spirit of criticism _________ am delivered now and the blood of Jesus Christ bears witness to my deliverance and salvation (1 John 5:8). In Jesus mighty name. Amen!

TESTIMONY: We overcome satan by the blood of the lamb and by the word of our testimony. Make sure that you testify to the glory of God and to the shame of satan. Pray for your testimony that as you pray it touches others and deliver them. Satan has been using you to fulfil his evil desires now let God use for the expansion of

His kingdom.

DELIVERANCE FROM THE SPIRIT OF MAMMON

(Matthew 6:24,19-21;1 Timothy 6:6-10,17; Hebrews 13:5; Psalms 62:10;Exodus 20:3)

The word Mammon means riches. The spirit of mammon says "You don't need God" You are Self Sufficient. You don't need God, trust in riches.

Money has a spirit on it. It either has the spirit of God or the spirit of mammon. Mammon is a spirit that tries to take the very place of God in your life. It promises you those things that only God can do or give- security, significance, identity, independence, power, freedom.

Money is not the root of all kinds of evil, but the love of money is a root of all kinds of evil. The spirit of mammon wants you to trust in money rather than God.

(Luke 15:11 -32) the spirit of mammon influenced the prodigal son to make poor decisions. It told him you have money, you don't need anyone, you are Mr Everything. It advised him to make a stupid decision, to leave home and go to a far country; foolishness indeed. The spirit of mammon will tell you that your budget is tight, don't pay tithes. The mammon spirit will tell you to get a loan and buy a car or build a house and use the money for tithing to pay the loan, it advises you "nicely" but at the end, you will cry. It will tell you to make a pledge and don't fulfil it. When he left the spirit of mammon was clapping hands for him saying I got you, boy. If you agree with the mammon spirit and buy a car, build a house or get a loan and marry and use tithes to pay, you will never enjoy that car, never finish building that house, you will marry but I won't be surprised if you divorce or have marital problems like childlessness. Mammon spirit is a spirit of waste. The prodigal son wasted all that he had with riotous living. If you let this spirit control you, waste will always follow you.

The spirit of mammon is the one that encourages people to cheat and steal at work, home and even in the church you steal money.

You steal from your husband, wife, children, and church even from the man of God. When you don't pay tithes don't you know you are stealing what God meant for his servant? You get increment at work then you don't tell your wife/husband, you get extra payment at work you hide it from your wife/husband, you don't even pay tithes. Mammon has taken control.

"If God finds that He cannot withdraw from you, He will stop depositing in you".

INSTRUCTIONS

- ✓ Pray between 12 midnight to 0400 hrs. This is time to intensify prayer
- ✓ Fast and pray for seven (7) days
  Day 1: from 12 midnight – 12 noon
  Day 2: from 12 midnight – 12 noon
  Day 3: from 12 midnight – 3 pm
  Day 4: from 12 midnight – 5 pm
  Day 5: from 12 midnight – 7 pm
  Day 6: from 12 midnight – 7 pm
  Day 7: from 12 midnight – 7 pm
- ✓ During the day, also pray

PRAYER POINTS

- ☐ Father, God! Forgive me for serving the spirit of mammon instead of serving you, the only true God.
- ☐ You spirit of mammon, I uproot you by your roots and overthrow you in the mighty name of Jesus Christ.
- ☐ I break all assignments of the devil against my finances in the mighty name of Jesus Christ.
- ☐ I break all curses of poverty, lack, debts and financial crisis that befell me as a result of obeying the mammon spirit in the mighty name of Jesus Christ.

CONFESSION OF FAITH

I brother/sister _________________ confess that on this ______ day of __________, I was delivered from the spirit of mammon, I am delivered now and the blood of Jesus Christ bears witness to my deliverance and salvation (1 John 5:8). In Jesus mighty name. Amen!

ACTIVATION PRAYER

I announce that it is You who have delivered and blessed me. The enemy wanted to destroy me with the spirit of mammon but you delivered me for when the enemy shall come in like a flood Your spirit lifts up a standard against him. I lift false burdens and remove feelings of heaviness, oppression and depression. I cast them upon the Lord, who sustains me. If it was not of you I would have been destroyed by mammon and powers of satan. I shall not be moved (Isaiah 10:27; 61:3; Psalms 12:5; John 14:1; Mathew 11:28-30)

PLEDGE OF FAITH

Father God, on this _______ day of _______________ I make a promise unto you, that I will always be a faithful tither and a cheerful, liberal giver. In the name of the Father, the Son and the Holy Spirit!

ACTION: Don't just pray, add action to your prayers. You have been limited, now you are trusting God for a breakthrough. It may be for your business, your plan to marry, career, finance etc. take a seed, by faith go and sow into the grace and anointing of your man of God. The man of God will pray for you and release uncommon favour, financial grace, favour for academic excellence, it will depend on what you want. Don't waste time act quickly. If you are still struggling with the spirit of mammon, selfishness, stinginess this will be difficult for you. Remember demons work in clusters.

TESTIMONY: We overcome satan by the blood of the lamb and by the word of our testimony. When God opens doors for you and gives you breakthrough make sure that you testify to the glory of His name and to the shame of satan. Pray for your testimony that as you testify it touches others and deliver them. satan has been using you to fulfil his evil desires now let God use you for the expansion of His kingdom.

DELIVERANCE FROM THE SPIRIT OF REGRETS

Regret may be defined as the stress of the mind, or a painful memory, over something that happened in the past. This refers to something that you did that lies beyond the possibility of repair, something that is beyond the scope of correction. Everyone experiences a certain amount of regret and shame over sins committed in the past or mistakes of the past.

Adam and Eve (Genesis 3:10) – after sinning against God they regretted. The felt the embarrassment and shame of sin. Maybe they thought God would not know. Like many of us, there are times we do things hoping that nobody will know but when everything gets exposed imagine the shame and embarrassment. Sometimes people may not know, it's only you who knows but the thing is eating you inside and tearing you apart. The only thing to do is to sit there shedding tears of regret. What are you regretting in your life that is robbing you of peace and your walk with God? When all hope is lost, turn to the Lord for mercy and grace.

Like Peter who denied the Lord, and was healed and restored, you too can be restored. John 13:37-38, 15-27; Mathew 26:31-35, Peter denied ever knowing Jesus. After he denied Christ, he went outside and wept bitterly – Luke 22:62. He was restored and established in the faith. Remove your eyes from your past mistakes and focus on Jesus Christ the author of your faith (Hebrews 12:2). Forget what is behind and strain toward what is ahead, press on toward the goal to win the prize for which God has called you heavenward in Christ Jesus (Philippians 3:13-14).

The sorrow that comes around by circumstances beyond one's control or power to repair an expression of distressing emotion (2 Corinthians 7:10; Matthew 27:3; 26:75). For how long are you going to be pondering over your past mistakes, crying and regretting. It happened, just accept that it happened.

Repent and depart from evil and allow the Lord to heal you and you shall be healed. If you can genuinely repent and forsake all your sins, the Lord will forgive you. The word of God says blessed is the man whose sins are forgiven and covered, and "there is now no condemnation for those who are in Christ Jesus"

INSTRUCTIONS

- ✓ Pray between 12 midnight to 0400 hrs. This is time to intensify prayer

✓ Fast and pray for three (3) days
  Day 1: from 12 midnight – 3 pm
  Day 2: from 12 midnight – 6 pm
  Day 3: from 12midnight – 12 midnight
✓ During the day, also pray

PRAYER POINTS

Father God! Forgive me for sinning against you. Please Lord, deliver me because of the sin I committed, I am full of fear and panic. I am not sure what I should expect next. I am afraid I may suffer the consequences of what I have done bitterly. I can't stand the shame and embarrassment this can bring into my life. Father God! Your word says "if I confess my sins, you are faithful and just to forgive me my sins, and to cleanse me from all unrighteousness" (1 John 1:9). Forgive me father, in the mighty name of Jesus Chris.

ACTIVATION PRAYER

I resist satanic contentions, intentions, provocations and negotiations concerning my life and soul, I bind satanic harassment and rebuke satanic concentrations meant to destroy my life in the mighty name of Jesus Christ. My father has forgiven me all my sins and there is now no condemnation over my life this I decree and declare in the mighty name of Jesus.

CONFESSION OF FAITH

I brother/sister ____________ confess that on this ______day of ____________, I was delivered from the spirit of regret, I am delivered now and the blood of Jesus Christ bears witness to my deliverance and salvation (1 John 5:8). In Jesus mighty name. Amen!

HOUSE CLEANSING

Before you try to cast out demons out of your house, find out what attracted them. If in your house you watch satanic movies and pornography demons will use that to enter. Bringing satanic objects, cursed objects in your house can be another doorway. When you are doing house cleansing make sure you get rid of everything that is satanic. Sometimes it may not be you bringing satanic things in the house but your children.

INSTRUCTIONS

- ✓ Pray between 12 midnight to 0400 hrs. This is time to intensify prayer
- ✓ Fast and pray for three (3) days
  Day 1: from 12 midnight – 3 pm
  Day 2: from 12 midnight – 6 pm
  Day 3: from 12midnight – 12 midnight
- ✓ During the day, also pray

PRAYER POINTS

- ☐ I soak the house from the roof to the ground in the blood of Jesus. The blood x 21
- ☐ I set this house ablaze with Holy Ghost Fire from the roof to the ground.
- ☐ I destroy every strange power in this house by the blood of Jesus.
- ☐ I consume evil spirit hiding in this house by the Holy Ghost Fire (7) times
- ☐ I destroy the satanic foundation that this house was built upon, receive divine earthquake and be destroyed.
- ☐ You demons assigned against this house, I torment you by Holy Ghost Fire-be tormented in the mighty name of Jesus Christ (say it as many times as you can). Demons of prayerlessness, heaviness whatever you are feeling in your house, fire, fire, the blood of Jesus, the blood of Jesus.
- ☐ Any charm buried in this yard receives lightning.
- ☐ Let the terror and destruction of God come suddenly upon any power that may want to attack me and my family as a result of these prayers.
- ☐ I decree and declare that as the mountains surround Jerusalem, the Lord has surrounded this house. The Lord is my wall of protection in this house.

DELIVERANCE FROM THE SPIRIT OF PRIDE

(PROVERBS 16:18)

Pride is a very stubborn demon. In Job 41, pride manifests itself

"

in the realm of the spirit as a leviathan, the crooked sea serpent. Spirits operating with the demonic cluster of pride include arrogance, haughtiness, puffed up, self –exaltation, vanity, rebellion, stubbornness, scorning, defiance and anti-submissiveness.

Pride brings destruction and a curse, causing a person to err (Psalms 119:21). God resists the proud (James 4:6). The fear of the Lord is to hate pride and arrogance (Proverbs 8:13). Pride is anti-prayer spirit. It blocks prayer and the moving of the Holy Spirit. It is a self-praiser spirit (Proverbs 27:2). The King of pride is leviathan (Job 41:1, 34).

Most people who have pride don't easily get deliverance because the king of pride's major job is to block deliverance. People who refuse to open up to the ministry of deliverance are being controlled by the leviathan spirit.

Pride causes;

- People to lean on their own understanding
- People to think that they don't need God or anyone
- People not to see the value in others
- People to compete instead of teaming up with others.

SYMPTOMS OF PRIDE

- Fault-finding
- A harsh spirit
- Defensiveness
- Accepting no responsibility for wrongdoing
- Desperation for attention
- Neglecting others
- Treating others unfairly

INSTRUCTIONS

- ✓ Pray between 12 midnight to 0400 hrs. This is time to intensify prayer
- ✓ Fast and pray for five (5) days
  Day 1: from 12 midnight – 12 noon
  Day 2: from 12 midnight – 12 noon
  Day 3: from 12 midnight – 3 pm
  Day 4: from 12 midnight – 6 pm

Day 5: from 12midnight – 12 midnight
✓ During the day, also pray

PRAYER POINTS

- ☐ I break all curses of pride and leviathan from my life.
- ☐ Let not the root of pride come against me (Psalms 36:11).
- ☐ I break the crown of pride (Isaiah 28:1).
- ☐ Father! according to your word, in his pride the wicked man does not seek you: in all his thoughts there is no room for you –Psalms 10:4
- ☐ Father, God! Help me to always make room in my thoughts for you. Don't allow me to continue in pride that stops me from seeking you! Keep me Christ minded; always casting my cares upon you. Lord, your word speaks of the wicked wearing pride like a necklace and clothing themselves with violence –Psalms 73:6
- ☐ Father, God! Deliver me from pride.
- ☐ Your word says when pride comes, then comes disgrace, but with humility comes wisdom (Proverbs 11:2; 13:13:10).
- ☐ Father! Grant me the grace to be humble and pour your wisdom upon me.
- ☐ Command the spirit of pride to come out of your life.
- ☐ Declare yourself free in the name of Jesus Christ.

CONFESSION OF FAITH

I brother/sister _____________ declare that on this_______ day of _______________, I was delivered from the spirit of pride, I am delivered now and the blood of Jesus Christ bears witness to my deliverance and salvation (1 John 5:8). In Jesus mighty name. Amen!

TESTIMONY: We overcome satan by the blood of the lamb and by the word of our testimony. Make sure that you testify to the glory of God and to the shame of satan. Pray for your testimony that as you testify it touches others and deliver them. Satan has been using you to fulfil his evil desires now let God use you for the expansion of His kingdom.

DELIVERANCE FROM THE SPIRIT OF NEGATIVE THINKING

Philippians 4:8-9; proverbs 23:7

WHAT IS NEGATIVE THINKING?

- Thinking about what you do not want.
- It is a way of thinking that brings pain into your life.
- It is a way of thinking that brings stress, fear, anxiety, worry and depression into your life.
- It is a way of thinking that works against you.
- It is a way of thinking that makes you feel bad, worse, defeated, worried and discouraged
- It is a way of thinking that hinders you to achieve what you want to achieve.

Nothing is going to change until you change the way you think.

What you focus on and constantly think is what you produce.

You must empty your mind of every negative thought.

Changing the way you think is making your mind to give you the good that you want.

EFFECTS OF NEGATIVE THOUGHTS

1. Negative thoughts poison the mind.

2. All negative thinking is fear-based.

3. You focus much on what you do not want.

4. They make you feel defeated.

5. Brings anxiety, worry, stress, depression etc.

6. They make you fail.

OVERCOMING NEGATIVE THINKING

We mentioned that;

- Nothing is going to change until you change the way you think.

☐ What you think about and constantly focus on is what you produce.

☐ Change requires effort and discipline.

☐ Changing the way you think is making your mind to give you the good that you want.

☐ Changing the way you think is to be in charge of your thought life (1 Corinthians 10:5).Matthew 19:16-22

The young man wanted to follow Jesus Christ but he did not want to depart from his old lifestyle.

☐ Your life is NOT going to change simply because you come to church.

☐ Do something to bring change into your life.

N.B –Changing your mind is to introduce a NEW PATTERN OF THINKING to your life (Romans 13:14; Ephesians 4:24; 1 Peter 2:11).

Your thoughts determine your feelings and your feelings determine your ACTION (Proverbs 23:7; Luke 6:45; Matthew 5:28).

WHEN A CHILD OF GOD START HAVING NEGATIVE THOUGHTS;

It is a sign of lack of faith (Hebrews 11:6; Proverbs 29:25).

Lack of faith gives birth to fear and fear gives birth to SIN (1 Corinthians 2:16). A thinker who has the mind of Christ has the ABILITY to resist Negative thoughts and replace them with godly thoughts.

HOW DO YOU CREATE A POSITIVE MINDSET?

1. Be born again

2. Have faith in God

3. Fill your mind with the word of God

Romans 10:17; Joshua 1:8

4. Talk to somebody –Eccl 4:9-10

5. Stop regretting

6. Don't give up –Micah 7:8; Matthew 11:28

7. Be militant –Matthew 11:12

8. Be aggressive

9. Create a refreshing atmosphere

10. Admit that mistakes do happen in life

11. Admit that in life things will not always go your way

12. Change the way you think

13. Stop feeling like nobody cares about you

14. Think about good things (Philippians 4:4-8)

  Be careful what you set your mind on because that is surely what you will become.

  Every time when you think is either you are positive or negative.

15. Avoid everything that can pollute your mind

CHECK;

    ☐ The music you listen to
    ☐ The movies you watch
    ☐ The books you read / magazines
    ☐ The shows you watch on TV
    ☐ The conversation you have at work, school etc.
    ☐ The text messages you send or receive
    ☐ Facebook communications and comments
    ☐ The places you go to
    ☐ Your secrets habits
    ☐ The people you associate with (1 Corinthians 15:33).

YOU ARE NOT WHAT YOU THINK YOU ARE, BUT WHAT YOU THINK - Proverbs 23:7

    ☐ Angry thoughts –angry works
    ☐ If you fill your mind with the sexual fantasies-your body will

find a way to fulfil them.
- ☐ If you dwell on your problems –they will defeat you.
- ☐ If you feel like a victim -soon you will be one.
- ☐ If you expect defeat you will be defeated

THE RENEWED MIND

- ☐ The renewed mind is a mind that is always subject to the word of God (Romans 8:5-9).
- ☐ It is easy to preach to people who always read the Bible (1 Corinthians 2:7, 14).
- ☐ We learned that for our minds to be cleansed we need to abide in the word of God (Matthew 5:28; 15:19; Proverbs 6:25; James 1:14-15).
- ☐ Also, we learned that prayer is a key to overcoming negativity (1 Peter 5:7; Philippians 4:6).

Ordinary prayers solve ordinary problems - Extraordinary prayers solve extraordinary problems

- ☐ (2 Corinthians 10:3-5) The battle of the Christians life is in the mind.
- ☐ Our thoughts become programmed over time to follow a specific pattern.
- ☐ God wants you to be delivered from mental strongholds.
- ☐ These are the thoughts which have been planted in our minds and they have become habits.

WHAT IS A RENEWED MIND?

- ☐ A mind that has been trained to think the truth (Colossians 3:10).
- ☐ You think as God thinks.
- ☐ You speak God's language.
- ☐ God's passion becomes your passion.
- ☐ His purposes become your purpose.

INSTRUCTIONS

- ✓ Pray between 12 midnight to 0400 hrs. This is time to intensify prayer
- ✓ Fast and pray for seven (7) days

Day 1: from 12 midnight – 12 noon
Day 2: from 12 midnight – 12 noon
Day 3: from 12 midnight – 3 pm
Day 4: from 12 midnight – 5 pm
Day 5: from 12 midnight – 7 pm
Day 6: from 12 midnight – 7 pm
Day 7: from 12 midnight – 7 pm
- ✓ During the day, also pray

PRAYER POINTS

- ➢ Father, deliver me from negative thoughts that bind me from having a positive life in the mighty name of Jesus.
- ➢ Father, cleanse my mind of all negativity by the power of your Holy Spirit in the mighty name of Jesus.
- ➢ Father, let this mind which was in Christ be in me in the mighty name of Jesus.
- ➢ I command all spirits to come out of mind control, confusion, forgetfulness, mental illness, double-mindedness and loss of memory to come out of mind in the mighty name of Jesus.
- ➢ I command all spirits of guilt, shame and condemnation to come out of my mind in the mighty name of Jesus.

CONFESSION OF FAITH

I brother/sister _________________ confess that on this ______ day of _____________, I was delivered from negative thoughts, I am delivered now and the blood of Jesus Christ bears witness to my deliverance and salvation (1 John 5:8). In Jesus mighty name. Amen!

TESTIMONY: We overcome satan by the blood of the lamb and by the word of our testimony. Make sure that you testify to the glory of God and to the shame of satan. Pray for your testimony that as you pray it touches others and deliver them. Satan has been using you to fulfil his evil desires now let God use you for the expansion of His kingdom.

DELIVERANCE FROM SATANIC SOUL TIES

A soul tie is a spiritual connection between two people who have been physically intimate with each other or who have had an intense

emotional or spiritual association. Soul ties are like super glue.

HOW ARE SOUL TIES FORMED?

- Close relationship
- Vows, commitment and promises
- Words of one's mouth

Statements such as;

- I will never stop loving you
- You will always be the only one I love
- I will never get you out of my heart
- You are the only one I will ever give my love to
- Nobody will ever take your place in my heart
- Sexual relationships

BREAKING SOUL TIES

1. Repent

Heavenly Father, I confess and repent of the sin of_______________________ and I ask you to forgive me.

2. Forgive

3. Break covenants

4. Get rid of gifts

5. Renounce and break the soul tie in Jesus Name.

INSTRUCTIONS

- ✓ Pray between 12 midnight to 0400 hrs. This is time to intensify prayer
- ✓ Fast from 12 midnight to 12 midnight (24 hrs.), 1-day prayer & fasting.
- ✓ During the day, also pray

I now renounce and lose myself from the ungodly soul tie which was formed between myself and you (name of the person)__________________through_____________ (activity/ event/ action/ words that lead to soul tie). (Name of the person)_________________ I take my life, heart and love from you. As I deeply breathe in and out am throwing your life out of my life (do it7x). As I spew and spit saliva out of my mouth I am removing everything that I inherited from you, that is now destroying my life (grief, sorrow, pain, rejection, accusation, limitation, hatred, hatred for men/ women etc.).

I decree and I declare with my mouth that there is no more soul tie between me and you_______________(Name of the person).

I now take authority and command any evil spirit which has taken advantage of this unholy soul tie to harass my life to come out in the mighty name of Jesus Christ.

CONFESSION

I brother/sister _____________declare that on this ____day of ________, I was delivered from the soul tie that was between me and _____________, I am now delivered and the blood of Jesus Christ bears witness to my deliverance and salvation (1 John 5:8). In Jesus mighty name. Amen!

DELIVERANCE FROM SEXUAL SINS

Sexual intercourse is one of the biggest weapons the enemy uses to hold people in bondage, captive to sin. Many can't just live without sex. Many Christians have found themselves in the bondage of sexual sins as they have been deceived by satan to think that they have to fulfil their desire for sex. Christians are called to live a holy life before their God. The truth is; all of us want to have sex, the devil knows it and therefore he would always try to push us into it. Sex is part of human life and thus many of us struggle with it, but it is a struggle that we can overcome.

We can't defeat sexual temptations in our own strength, but with God's help all things are possible (Mark 9:23; 10:27; 2 Corinthians 5:17)

The Bible tells us that our bodies are the temple of God (1 Corinthians 3:16) so we have to stay pure before God. To live a holy life is not something easy. It requires commitment, perseverance, self-control, self-discipline and self-motivation.

LUST

Lust can be a very powerful and gripping thing in a person's life. Often you will find yourself doing things you don't even want to do because the spiritual push is so strong to battle against. It is frustrating sometimes almost not being in control of your own body and even mind as you become consumed with this very strong and gripping spirit (Romans 7:14-16).

Identify when a desire bends from that of a healthy appreciation of another and becomes something more 'gripping'. Unhealthy sexual desires often happen when we try to fill a natural spiritual desire for something else with a sexual one. When a natural healthy desire tends to run away from you, two things need to happen. RUNAWAY from the sin. There are some sins we can face on with prayer and self-will, but this one area is definitely NOT the case. Simply avoid situations where you would be tempted, then you will be able to battle against this. You will notice that the same voice that tempts you to sin is the same voice that condemns you for sinning after you are done.

DELIVERED FROM THE GUILT OF SEXUAL SINS

Guilt from past sins and current sins are only intended to lead us to the point of repentance. If you have asked God for the forgiveness of a particular sin and you don't feel forgiven or you still feel the guilt, then this is bondage from the enemy as God is a loving and forgiving God, and he will NOT hold you against past sins after repentance. The guilt will only bring you down the same dark path again if you let it.

SEXUAL BONDAGES

You can't stop sexual desires from coming to your mind or even body however you can stop those desires from growing from just a desire/thought to becoming sexual sin. Sexual intercourse is a good gift from God (Genesis 2:24 -25; Proverbs 5:18-20). All sexual bondages can be broken through the power of the blood of Jesus. If you have been in the bondage of sexual desires, I want you to know that there is hope for you (Romans 6:14; 8:2). As you are going to conduct Self-Deliverance, pray sincerely out of a contrite heart and

God almighty will set you free from the chains of sexual perversion. If at all the yoke of sexual sins is going to be broken in your life you must be ready to fight for your life (Mathew 11:12). The sin that you don't stop will stop you. What you don't address today, will undress you tomorrow. An enemy that is not confronted is an enemy that has been given a residence permit. Each time you sin, you sink. Sexual sins are too bad because they open doors for all kinds of the evil spirit to enter your life.

SPIRITUAL CONTAMINATION FROM SEXUAL SINS – EXODUS 20:5; LEVITICUS 5:17

God wants to deliver you from spiritual contamination from past sexual sins, present sexual lusts, enticements and other sexual sins (Romans 1:22; 1:18-32; Leviticus 18:1-30). He wants you to be free from satanic deposits acquired by sleeping with demonized people and deposits acquired by sleeping with prostitutes (1 Corinthians 6:15 – 18)when a person has sex with another, whomever they have sex with, they get joined together with that person and the two become one flesh. The word of God forbids us to have sex outside marriage.

If you have had sex outside marriage, I want you to know that you must be delivered from sexual contamination. When you have sex it could result in you having sexually transmitted diseases or unwanted pregnancy. God cannot be mocked for whatever a person sows they are sure to reap. As Christians, we know that sex outside marriage is sin.

If we commit sexual sins and still believe that we are headed to heaven, we are lying to ourselves and greatly deceived to believe that we can do such things and not pay a penalty for our sins. 1 John 5:18, everyone who is born again does not keep on sinning. They might stumble and fall but a true believer will rise and get back to the Lord quickly. Proverbs 6:27, "can a man carry fire next to his chest and his clothes not be burned", sex before marriage is like putting fire on your chest. A person who is committing sexual sins is playing with fire. When you have sex with a person there is a transference of spirits that takes place. This is the contamination that you must be delivered from. When you sleep with a demonized person you will get demons from them. That is if that person carries demons of accidents, after sleeping with him/her accidents will follow you if he/she carries failure after sleeping with her everything in your life will collapse. If the demons afflicted the person with sickness be sure you will have your package. That's why some people were doing well in life, but after they met with a particular sin partner everything fell apart and no wonder if they go to witchdoctors they will be told the person is bewitching them. That person is not bewitching you, you become one, one flesh. Some people are sexually satanically anointed. If their spirits are strong they take what you have. Some people can't get married now because of what they got from their sexual partners.

If you have had sex outside marriage or before marriage, take stock of your life. Ask the Holy Spirit to minister to you. Why are things happening the way they are happening in your life?

Go to the Lord in prayer for deliverance and cleansing.

FORNICATION

Fornication is generally consensual sexual intercourse between two people who are not married to each other. It means to commit illicit sexual intercourse. It means unlawful sexual intercourse (1 Corinthians 6:18-20; 7:1-2). The Bible tells us to flee fornication (Psalms 145:17-21). God is righteous in His ways. When God says we must flee fornication and abstain from all sexual sins, He is not denying us anything good but he wants us to enjoy the proper sexual relationship in the proper time in marriage. If you obey the word of God and flee fornication and glorify God in your body, He will bless you. Sex, as God intended, is very good, but fornication is wrong and we must abstain from it. We must respect Gods word (2 Corinthians 7:14).

The church cannot win battles against satan if there is sin in the church (1 Corinthians 5:1-13). Somebody said a ship in the water is fine, but water in the ship can be disastrous. The Corinthian church tolerated sin and Paul the Apostle had to rebuke them. If you have been living in fornication, recognize your own sin, confess it, repent of it and forsake it (1 John 1:9). If you refuse to stop sin, you will soon feel the chastening of the Lord (Hebrews 12:5-11). God has provided a way of escape (1 Corinthians 10:13). Walk with God, avoid the very appearance of evil, seek His face in prayer, read and obey his word and you will overcome fornication.

HOW TO BE DELIVERED/ESCAPE

Admit/agree that fornication is sin

The Bible is very clear on this matter, it is not a matter of debate, fornication is sin and they that do it cannot inherit the kingdom of God. Fornicators can't enter heaven (1 Corinthians 6:9). They will all go to hell if they don't repent and be born again. If you have been living in fornication, repent, confess and forsake the sin of fornication and receive mercy and grace from the Lord for your salvation.

Flee - (1 Thessalonians 4:3; Acts 15:20; 1 Corinthians 6:18). The word of God tells us to flee fornication. The word flee means; to run away, to escape from, to disappear quickly, to vanish, to run away as from danger or evil, to hasten off. When you see fornication run away, disappear quickly. Children of God have the spirit of discernment, unless if you are a hypocrite. When a brother/sister in the church is been led by the spirit of satan to tempt you, you will know. Why should a brother/sister ask you to visit, to go and iron for him, why should a sister ask you to come and help her fix something and instruct you to come alone, why should the two of you go and do school work together, only the two of you? It is crystal clear, fornication. Why should a brother/sister phone in the middle of the night, what woke him up? Why is it that you and this brother/sister you are always together either at the mall, on Facebook or WhatsApp? You know the answer. Runaway from danger. Joseph ran for his life, Samson did not, he thought he was strong, he fell into the temptation and the glory of God left him.

If you meet a man/woman and the spirit of fornication begins to talk, you will know. You are a child of God you have the spirit of God. No matter how much they pretend to be nice or to be looking for help. If a man/woman wants to give you a lift, asking for your cell phone number etc. refuse, flee, escape for your life. Keep away from evil. Don't allow any man/woman/brother or sister to touch you in a way that arouses you sexually. Some of these people are possessed by demons, if you let them touch you in that manner they will transfer demons into your life (Ephesians 4:27), the word of God warns us not to give satan any chance.

Resist satan (James 4:7; Mathew 4:1- 4)

The devil will try to use your needs to tempt you, but whatever be the case put your trust in God. He tried to tempt our Lord, Jesus resisted him and came out victoriously. Whenever satan tempts you God will provide a way of escape. The fact that you don't have money or you are in need of something does not mean you should give your life to satan. You may be looking for a job and the manager promises to employ you only if you can sleep with him, refuse. Don't use sex as a qualification, if to them it's a requirement tell them your company is cursed and flee, run away, escape for your life.

Resist Peer Pressure

Don't allow your peers to push you, you want to have sex. Some of you, your greatest motivator is not your brethren nor the word of God but your peers out there. Don't allow your peers to cause you to sin against God. Don't let the music, movies and people around you encourage you to go against God. At the end of the day, you will stand alone on the day of judgement to give an account of what you did with your body. Sometimes to be able to please God you will have to distance yourself from some people you used to hang out with.

Talk to someone

If you realise that you have a challenge with overcoming fornication talk to somebody you feel you can trust. Sometimes it is good to open up to somebody. Remember two is better than one. Think of the consequences of fornication.

Pray

When you pray God will give you wisdom, strength and the power to always be on your guard. Mathew 26:41. Pray so that you may not fall into temptations.

Don't visit someone of the opposite sex alone

1 Thessalonians 5: 22.the word of God says that we should abstain from every form of evil, keep away from the appearance of evil. If a man/woman asks you to visit them refuse. They ask for your cell phone number refuse. Don't visit a brother/sister and start quoting scripture "God has given us the spirit of self-control "it does not work that way. Keep away from the appearance of evil. You go and spend the night at the brother's/sisters house and you say you will speak in tongues, if your tongues did not stop you and failed to prevent you from going to his/her house when you are there what can your tongues do. Can't you see they are weak like you? "The spirit indeed is willing but the flesh is weak "Mathew 26:41. So your flesh is strong? Don't deceive yourself, keep away.

ACTIVATION PRAYER

I speak to my DNA and declare that I am free from any and all influences passed down from one generation to another, biologically, socially, emotionally, psychologically, spiritually or by any other channel unknown to me, but known to God. I resist every spirit that acts as a gatekeeper or doorkeeper to my soul in the mighty name of Jesus Christ.

I open myself to divine deliverance, Father, have your way now!

INSTRUCTIONS

- ✓ Pray between 12 midnight to 0400 hrs. This is time to intensify prayer
- ✓ Fast and pray for five (5) days
  Day 1: from 12 midnight – 12 noon
  Day 2: from 12 midnight – 12 noon
  Day 3: from 12 midnight – 3 pm
  Day 4: from 12 midnight – 6 pm
  Day 5: from 12midnight – 12 midnight
- ✓ During the day, also pray.

PRAYER POINTS

- ☐ I command you the spirit of (e.g. fornication) _____________ to come out of my sexual character in the mighty name of

Jesus Christ.
- ☐ I command all spirits operating in my sexual organs to come out in the mighty name of Jesus Christ.
- ☐ I command the spirit of sexual addiction and sexual appetite to come out of my life in the mighty name of Jesus Christ.

CONFESSION

I decree and declare that I brother/sister _____________ on this _____ day of _____________ I was delivered from the spirit of fornication and the Holy Spirit bears witness for my salvation and deliverance.

In the name of the Father, the Son and The Holy Spirit I am free.

MASTURBATION

What is masturbation?

Masturbation is the stimulation of one's own genitals for sexual arousal usually with the hand for sexual pleasure and in a way that often climaxes in orgasm. The stimulation may also involve sex toys.

Is masturbation a Sin?

I have read articles concerning masturbation written by men and women of God. Some say masturbation is sin, some say it is not a sin and some say both. They say it depends on how one does it. In (Mathew 5:27-30), Jesus Christ speaks against having lustful thoughts. Now if lustful thoughts, looking at a woman and desiring her is sin, how about the act of satisfying those lustful thoughts? Masturbation is the result of lustful thoughts. I want you to follow the word of God with me here carefully. Jesus says, "But I say unto you, that whosoever looketh on a woman to lust after her hath committed adultery with her already in his heart. How does it happen in the heart? You imagine yourself kissing the woman, on the bed together etc. By so doing you have not gone into the actual act with the woman but you just did visualisation, but now listen, Jesus says you have already committed adultery, sin. (James 1:14) says everyone is tempted when he is drawn away of his own lust and enticement. Read verse 15 carefully, when lust is conceived it bringeth forth sin. When you spend time imagining like that, sexual desires become too strong in such a way that it will push you to look for a woman to go into the very act with, you will be burning with sexual desires. Now if there is no woman around to satisfy that desire the last resort will be to masturbate. Remember masturbation is the result of lustful thoughts.

Now how can masturbation not be a sin? **MASTURBATION IS A SIN.** Don't listen to these preachers who say masturbation is not a sin. They dilute the word of God for you to make you happy. If you continue masturbating, you will go to hell and burn in the lake of fire. Stop it, repent and be forgiven. Don't allow false teachers to send you to hell fire. The last part of verse 15 says 'and sin, when it is finished, bringeth forth death. Death here is separation from God, spiritual death. Sin brings spiritual death. After Adam and Eve sinned against God they died spiritually. They were separated from God. Satan told them they won't die if they ate the forbidden fruit, he told them eating the forbidden fruit was not sin, like people who are saying masturbation is not sin. (1 Corinthians 10:31), before you masturbate do you pray and give God the glory? The answer is obvious, you don't and you can't. Then what does this tell you? MASTURBATION IS SIN.

HOW TO BE DELIVERED

- Admit that masturbation is sin.
- Make a decision to stop it.
- Repent and receive grace and mercy from the Lord Jesus Christ for your salvation and deliverance.
- Ask God to renew your mind.
- If you have been watching pornography stop it immediately.
- Follow Self-Deliverance procedure and engage in serious spiritual warfare against the spirit of masturbation.

INSTRUCTIONS

- ✓ Pray between 12 midnight to 0400 hrs. This is time to intensify prayer
- ✓ Fast and pray for seven (7) days
  Day 1: from 12 midnight – 12 noon
  Day 2: from 12 midnight – 12 noon
  Day 3: from 12 midnight – 3 pm

Day 4: from 12 midnight – 5 pm
Day 5: from 12 midnight – 7 pm
Day 6: from 12 midnight – 7 pm
Day 7: from 12 midnight – 7 pm
✓ During the day, also pray

PRAYER POINTS

- Every inherited demon of sexual perversion in my life I command you, come out of my life in the mighty name of Jesus Christ.
- You demons of masturbation assigned to destroy my life I bind and cast you out of my life in the mighty name of Jesus Christ.
- Every sexual gate of masturbation opened in my life I shut you down and I command the gate of righteousness to open so that I may enter in (Psalms 118:19).
- You satanic powers of imaginations polluting my thought life be consumed by Holy Ghost fire and I release the power and the authority of the Lord against you (Mathew 10:1) in the mighty name of Jesus Christ.
- I uproot and cast out every spirit of masturbation planted in my sexual organ, my fingers and my hands in the mighty name of Jesus Christ.
- I release myself from every pollution of sexual sins in the mighty name of Jesus Christ.

CONFESSION OF FAITH

I decree and declare that I brother/sister __________ on this _____ day of __________ I was delivered from the spirit of masturbation and the Holy Spirit bears witness for my salvation and deliverance.

In the name of the Father, the Son and The Holy Spirit I am free.

DELIVERANCE FROM THE SPIRIT OF PROCRASTINATION

Ecclesiastes 11:4; Proverbs 18:9

What does the bible tell us about procrastination?

Procrastination is the habit of needless delaying where the action is required (Luke 9:59-62; James 4:17; John 9:4). You are a student, you are supposed to be studying then you choose to be on Facebook, you are a worker in the church you are supposed to be praying in preparation for Sunday service then you choose to watch a movie, instead of doing the right thing you go for the wrong thing, I call it wrong though it may not be a bad thing because at that particular time it is not what you are supposed to be doing. Then you keep on saying I will, I will, I will phone them, I will apply until it's late.

Procrastination is an enemy to success (Proverbs 12:24; 20:4; 13:4) If you have made procrastination your habit you will never have anything in life. The sluggard craves and gets nothing, while the soul of the diligent is richly supplied. You have long said you want to register a company, you want to start a business, you want to write books, you want to further your studies, how far have you gone? If you want to prosper and be successful in life, then you must overcome the spirit of procrastination. Procrastination drives away opportunities; it is an opportunity killer. Luke 9:59-62, these young men lost the opportunity to serve the master because of procrastination. How many of us have lost opportunities because of excuses? Procrastination is the act or practice of pulling off important tasks to a later time, choosing to do something else instead of the task you know you should be doing. Procrastination is a destroyer of blessings. It can rob your self-confidence, reliability and personal peace (Proverbs 18:9).

REASONS FOR PROCRASTINATION

- Laziness, lazy people want much but get little – (Proverbs 13:4; 18:9), they are great wasters. (Proverbs 6:6) Laziness is a sin. A lazy person hates work, his hands refuse to work. He loves to sleep, he gives excuses (Proverbs 21:25; 26:14: 13; 18:9). He believes he is wise but is a fool. The sluggard is wise in his own eyes than seven men who answer discreetly – Proverbs 26:16). A lazy person becomes a servant, "diligent hands will rule, but laziness ends in slave labour (Proverbs 12:24)". "A sluggard does not plough in season, so at harvest time he looks but finds nothing, but the soul of the diligent shall be made rich" (Proverbs 13:4). there is no room for laziness in the life of a Christian.

☐ Fear, the fear of man is a trap (Proverbs 29:25). You say I will preach to him, fear says later, you say I want to marry, fear says later and you keep on postponing until you can't do it anymore. Decisions that are influenced by fear never come to pass. Fear will make you live a life of running away. Fear will prevent you from moving forward in life. What is scaring you in your life that keeps on making you postpone your plans? Don't you think it's time to run towards that Goliath? Have confidence in God and run towards that Goliath that is scaring your life. Refuse to be intimidated (Psalms 56:3; 1 Samuel 17:48). Take courage and confront that devil and cast him out of your way. (Psalms 34:4; 1 John 4:18; Psalms 91:3) wait, what are you fearing? You are scared to buy yourself a car because you think witches will bewitch you. (2 Timothy 1:12-17), God has not given you a spirit of fear but of power and remember, the righteous are as bold as a lion (Proverbs 28:1).

☐ Doubt/uncertainty (James 1:8), a double-minded man is unstable in all he does, you can't know what really he wants in life. He is confused and everything he does end up in confusion or destruction. He does not keep promises. He wants to do many things at one time and normally he ends up losing everything. He starts and he never finishes, even when he starts you know he won't finish. How many people have been saying I am marrying, are they married? I am starting this and that, did they start?

☐ Wrong Association (2 Timothy 2:16-26; 1 Corinthians 15:33) Stay away from foolish useless talks because that will lead you away from God, it will cast you out of your destiny. Keep away from useless people. Their evil useless and foolish talk will enter you and spread like a sickness inside your body. If you continue associating with them they will destroy your faith, they will mislead you. They are destiny killers. When you see them coming run away, run very fast. Runaway from the evil they like to do. Stay away from foolish and stupid discussions and arguments (Ephesians 5:11), do not have fellowship with the unfruitful works of darkness. If you hang around them, you will become useless and die uselessly. These are the people you interact with regularly at work, school, church or wherever. When you distance yourself from negative people and replace them with positive supportive people this will help you to be stable and have a focus in life.

By their fruits you will know them – they gossip, they spend much time uselessly on social media, they are always after pleasure, they don't listen to good teachings, they are rebellious, always talking about girls/boys, they are into drugs etc. The only thing you can do is to pray for them and share the gospel of Jesus Christ with them.

☐ SIN – Sin is a destiny killer. It will make you stagnant. When you are a slave of sin nothing moves for good in your life. You live a life of crying, disappointments, regrets, frustration, failure, limitation, stagnation and pain. Sin is the enemy of success. The devil will use sin to delay you, to keep you moving in circles and bring failure into your life. He can come in the form of the lust of the flesh, pride of life, love for money and lack of self-control and many other things he may find fit to use to destroy you. Instead of going forward in your life satan will use sin to keep you back and by the time you realise, time would have been far much spent. satan knows how to delay you. He can use girls/women to hinder you to marry, you will keep on saying I want to marry. Sin will destroy your life. Repent and come out of sin. Don't wait until it is late. Come to Jesus Christ for your salvation.

HOW TO BE DELIVERED

1. Acknowledge the problem (Proverbs 21:25).

2. Ask for wisdom (Ecclesiastes 8:6; James 1:5).

3. Plan to change (Ecclesiastes 3:17; Proverbs 28:17).

4. Ask for help when you feel stuck (Proverbs 12:5).

5. Keep away from wrong associates

6. Avoid laziness

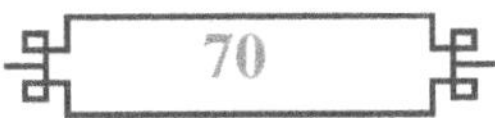

7. Overcome fear

INSTRUCTIONS

- ✓ Pray between 12 midnight to 0400 hrs. This is time to intensify prayer
- ✓ Fast and pray for five (5) days
  Day 1: from 12 midnight – 12 noon
  Day 2: from 12 midnight – 12 noon
  Day 3: from 12 midnight – 3 pm
  Day 4: from 12 midnight – 6 pm
  Day 5: from 12midnight – 12 midnight
- ✓ During the day, also pray.

PRAYER POINTS

- Let every plant of procrastination planted in my life be rooted out in the mighty name of Jesus Christ
- Father, God! Stretch out your arm and deliver me from the bondage of procrastination-Exodus 6:6 in the mighty name of Jesus Christ
- You spirit of procrastination, I release the sword of the Lord against you – Judges 7:18, in the mighty name of Jesus Christ.
- I break fear, the power of sin, laziness and any other thing that is the cause of procrastination in my life and I command them to come out of my life in the mighty name of Jesus Christ.
- You spirit of procrastination, I take authority over you, from today you will have no control over my life, die and never resurrect in the mighty name of Jesus Christ.
- I decree and declare that I am free from the devil of procrastination.
- My life is flourishing like a tree planted by the riverside
- I have supernatural energy to Walk the journey of my life
- Superhero speed is mine and I am overtaking
- I am not the tail, I am the head
- The Lord is the strength of my life – Psalms 27:1

ACTIVATION PRAYER

I decree that this day I operate according to Gods divine timetable/ calendar. I decree that God's agenda is my agenda.

I decree and declare that my times and seasons are in the hands of the Lord and they shall not be altered by anything. I function under the anointing of the sons of Issachar and God gives me the divine ability to be able to accurately discern my times and seasons, in the mighty name of Jesus Christ.

CONFESSION OF FAITH

I decree and declare that I brother/sister __________ on this ____ day of __________ I was delivered from the spirit of procrastination and the Holy Spirit bears witness for my salvation and deliverance.

In the name of the Father, the Son and The Holy Spirit I am free.

TESTIMONY: We overcome satan by the blood of the lamb and by the word of our testimony. Make sure that you testify to the glory of God and to the shame of satan. Pray for your testimony that as you testify it touches others and deliver them. Satan has been using you to fulfil his evil desires now let God use for the expansion of His kingdom.

CHAPTER 4
DELIVERANCE FROM THE SPIRIT OF ANTI - MARRIAGE

Anti-Marriage is a spirit that fights against marriage. It is the spirit responsible for hindering people from getting married. It is a spirit responsible for breaking relationships. For those who are married the spirit will stir up quarrels and contentions which might lead to divorce. If a man or woman is under the influence of this spirit, he/she is prone to experience extramarital affairs and unfaithfulness.

Sometimes you find yourself under this spirit due to ancestral altars. For example, a vow may be made by parents on behalf of their children and they will not get married as a result. This spirit also works in dreams; where you start to see yourself sleeping and having sex in the dream which means you are having a spiritual husband/wife.

It also works through accusations. One spouse may accuse the other or they may both accuse each other of extramarital affairs. Accusations can also break relationships that were meant for marriage. These accusations also have the spirit of suspicion which destroys trust in marriages. This spirit works through the spirit of rejection. That is why some marriage proposals are never successful. Even if they can be given a positive answer it is bound to break quickly.

This spirit is also encompassed by the spirit of selfishness with the connotation that they don't want to share their possession/ money with other people. They feel a person will be ripping them off their money.

This spirit also takes advantage of spirits that are already working in the lives of people e.g. pride whereby a lady/man who wants to get married is puffed up and pompous thinking that they belong to a higher and better class and this hinders them from getting married.

Sometimes people don't get married because their families are cursed with an anti-marriage spirit and this manifests by a woman having children with different men. No one proposes and usually, if they get married they end up in divorce. This can be due to witchcraft. satan hates marriages.

OPERATION OF ANTI-MARRIAGE ALTARS

In some families, their daughters never marry or late marriage or must divorce, some they don't give birth; some don't have more than one child, some die at a particular age after marrying and some remain unmarried or childless. The cases are endless and indicate anti-marriage altars in operation.

Anti-marriage spirit can also manifest itself through health issues or bad habits. Some families struggle with alcoholism, womanising, lies and childlessness.

INSTRUCTIONS

- ✓ Pray between 12 midnight to 0400 hrs. This is time to intensify prayer
- ✓ Fast and pray for seven (7) days
  Day 1: from 12 midnight – 12 noon
  Day 2: from 12 midnight – 12 noon
  Day 3: from 12 midnight – 3 pm
  Day 4: from 12 midnight – 5 pm
  Day 5: from 12 midnight – 7 pm
  Day 6: from 12 midnight – 7 pm
  Day 7: from 12 midnight – 7 pm
- ✓ During the day, also pray

PRAYER POINTS

- ☐ I raise a divine injection against all gatherings that are not unto the Lord, warring against my family, in the name of Jesus Christ.
- ☐ Every evil altar erected against my marriage in the witchcraft coven is dismantled by fire, in the name of Jesus.
- ☐ Any power that wants to make me a permanent candidate of

marital failure, release me and die, in the name of Jesus.

- ☐ Every witchcraft power of my father's house, witchcraft power of my mother's house, witchcraft power of my in-law's house, I summon you together: Be destroyed by fire in the name of Jesus.
- ☐ I paralyze every evil leg walking in and out of my marriage, in the name of Jesus.
- ☐ I decree by the power in the blood of Jesus: Let the glory of my marriage be restored, in the name of Jesus.
- ☐ I break every covenant of marital failure and late marriage in the mighty name of Jesus Christ.
- ☐ I destroy every evil force magnetizing the wrong people to me, be paralyzed in the mighty name of Jesus Christ
- ☐ I command all forces of evil manipulation and delay which are hindering my marriage, be completely paralyzed in the mighty name of Jesus Christ.
- ☐ I command all evil anti-marriage marks be removed from my life in the mighty name of Jesus Christ
- ☐ I decree and declare that I am delivered from anti-marriage altar and I shall not miss my wedding date in the mighty name of Jesus Christ.

ACTIVATION PRAYER

I decree and declare divine judgement against anti-marriage altar and its activities. I disapprove, nullify, dismantle, cancel and forcefully oppose any anti-marriage altar operations, manipulations, strategies, tactics, plots and plans which are designed to hinder or prevent me to marry/get married and which are designed to delay Gods original plans and purposes in their correct time and season in the mighty name of Jesus Christ.

CONFESSION

I decree and declare that I brother/sister ______________ on this ____ day of ______________ I was delivered from **anti-marriage altar** and the Holy Spirit bears witness for my salvation and deliverance. In the name of the Father, the Son and The Holy Spirit I am free.

PRAYING FOR A LIFE PARTNER

Being single can be hard at times. It can be challenging watching couples embracing one another. It can be lonely. Adam was lonely, that's why God made Eve for him (Genesis 2:18). It is a godly thing to want to have a life partner. Identifying who to marry is an important part of your life. It is one of the major decisions of life. You can go to many people and attend marriage seminars on how to identify a life partner but the only opinion that matters is Gods. This is why it is crucial that we take marriage to God in prayer before and after marrying.

PRAYER - BROTHER

Father, God! You declared in your word that it is not good for a man to be alone (Genesis 2:18). Father, I ask you to lead me to the sister you have prepared and chosen for me to be my wife. While I am waiting for you to reveal her to me to help me to know myself better. Help me to address those areas of my life which are not of the order of your will and your word which will interfere and hinder me to have a successful marriage when I finally get married.

Give me the grace to keep away from fornication to keep myself pure for the sister I am going to marry soon.

Father give me the grace to overcome sexual temptations. I want to keep myself pure and safe for my wife. Help me Lord not to sleep with any woman who is not my wife. Give me the grace to flee fornication and the lust of the flesh.

Father keep that sister safe so that no one takes her. Open my eyes Lord so that I may behold my beloved. Lead me, Lord, direct me and order my steps. You know the longing of my heart and you know what is best for me.

Lord, I place my trust in you in identifying a life partner, in the mighty name of Jesus.

PRAYER - SISTER

Father, I so desperately desire to have a husband. I trust in you and I know you have my interest in mind. My delight is in you Lord. I bring my heart desire to get married to you. Please, Lord! Grant me my heart desire (Psalms 37:4). Father, you made Eve and you brought her to Adam. I ask you to open the spiritual eyes of the brother you have been preparing me for, so that he may see me. Prepare his heart and my own so that when we find each other we will know that this is the Lords doing and it is marvellous in our eyes. Father give me the grace to overcome sexual temptations. I want to keep myself pure and safe for my husband. Help me Lord not to sleep with any man who is not my husband. Give me the grace to flee fornication and the lust of the flesh.

Help me, Father, to keep myself pure until the wedding day, give me strength when I feel weak. While am waiting to give me the grace to endure each day, in the mighty name of Jesus.

DELIVERANCE FROM THE SERPENTINE ALTARS

Leviathan is a serpent-like creature. Leviathan works like python. Leviathan is not a demon but a principality (Job 40 & 41; Proverbs 6:16-19; revelation 12:3). This marine monster stops growth, hinders spiritual growth, stops gifts of the Holy Spirit and it is the cause of people's inability to speak in tongues.

Serpentine spirits get their powers from Leviathan, so when dealing with them we must know that we are dealing with Leviathan himself. To overthrow Leviathan, the word of God must be aggressively read against him, hailstone, coals of fire, thunder, lightning, seaquake, air quake and earthquake must be released against these powers to destroy them.

INSTRUCTIONS

- ✓ Pray between 12 midnight to 0400 hrs. This is time to intensify prayer
- ✓ Fast and pray for five (5) days
     Day 1: from 12 midnight – 12 noon
     Day 2: from 12 midnight – 12 noon
     Day 3: from 12 midnight – 3 pm
     Day 4: from 12 midnight – 6 pm
     Day 5: from 12midnight – 12 midnight
- ✓ During the day, also pray

PRAYER POINTS

- [] My father, my father, break the heads of leviathan in pieces in the mighty name of Jesus Christ – (Psalms 74:14).
- [] My father, my God, punish leviathan, the piercing serpent, even leviathan the crooked serpent, with your sore, great and strong sword in the mighty name of Jesus Christ – Isaiah 27:1.
- [] I break all and I slay all curses of leviathan from my life in the mighty name of Jesus Christ .
- [] Almighty God, rip the scales of leviathan so that I may experience revival and the manifestation of the gifts of the Holy Spirit in my life – Job 41:15, in the mighty name of Jesus Christ.
- [] I put a hook in leviathan's nose, a cord around his tongue and I release hailstones, coals of fire, thunder and seaquake all over him in the mighty name of Jesus Christ – Job 41:1-2
- [] I decree and declare that I am free from curses of leviathan and every sea monster in the mighty name of Jesus Christ.
- [] I am free from serpentine altars in the mighty name of Jesus Christ.

CONFESSION OF FAITH

I decree and declare that I brother/sister ______________ on this ____day of ______________I was delivered from the serpentine spirit and the Holy Spirit bears witness for my salvation and deliverance.

In the name of the Father, the Son and The Holy Spirit I am free.

TESTIMONY: We overcome satan by the blood of the lamb and by the word of our testimony. Make sure that you testify to the glory of God and the shame of satan. Pray for your testimony that as you testify it touches others and deliver them. Satan has been using you to fulfil his evil desires now let God use you for the expansion of His kingdom.

DELIVERANCE FROM ANCESTRAL ALTARS

Ancestral altars are altars dedicated to the worship of demons (Exodus 20:1-5; 1 Samuel 28:3). These altars operate through familiar spirits. Familiar spirits are spirits that have attached themselves to people due to legal grounds given to them by their forefathers (Deuteronomy 18:10-11; Jeremiah 27:9-10). Altars are spiritual things. An Ancestral altar is a place of a spiritual link between the supernatural and the people anchored on the covenant (Leviticus 17:5-7).

WHAT IS AN ANCESTRAL ALTAR?

Every family has a history. Your family originated from somewhere. There is something your parents worshipped/worship. It is an altar that deals with the foundation of your family. How your family started or how its foundation was laid. It has to do with your family lineage. Ancestral altars operate through familiar spirits. Why do people end up like their parents? Ancestral altars. Check your life. These are spirits which have attached themselves to people because of legal rights given to them by their parents (Deuteronomy 18:10-11; Jeremiah 27:9-10).

EFFECTS OF AN ANCESTRAL ALTAR

- It opposes God's grace in your life

- It causes endless struggles and sufferings
- It opens doors for evil spirits
- It causes stagnation and limitation
- It causes poverty, divorce, shame, disgrace and conflicts
- Delay progress
- Influences to make wrong decisions in life

HOW TO DESTROY ANCESTRAL ALTAR

Destroying altars is not a child's play. Evil altars are not supposed to be taken lightly. Altar breaking prayers are dangerous prayers. It takes an altar to destroy an altar-you must have a strong personal altar in order to destroy satanic altars. You must be connected to the altar of your man of God. It takes a sacrifice to be connected to an altar. If you have never taken a sacrifice to the altar of your man of God, then his altar does not know you. The altar of your man of God covers you in situations whereby you can't fight any more and it seems like the enemy is overtaking. Some people just say God of my father, God of Apostle. Are you connected (2Chronicles 20:20)

In destroying altars, you need to be led by the Holy Spirit.

Know what your fathers were involved in during their time –what did they worship. These are some of the things to consider when dealing with Ancestral altars

How is your life? Take stock of your life. It is time that you disconnect yourself. Are you ready to destroy your father's altars? Gideon did. Judges 6:25-26. It is not easy to destroy or pull down satanic altars of the father's house but because you are anointed with power and fire you are well able. Fear not.

INSTRUCTIONS

- ✓ Pray between 12 midnight to 0400 hrs. This is time to intensify prayer
- ✓ Fast and pray for seven (7) days
  Day 1: from 12 midnight – 12 noon
  Day 2: from 12 midnight – 12 noon
  Day 3: from 12 midnight – 3 pm
  Day 4: from 12 midnight – 5 pm
  Day 5: from 12 midnight – 7 pm
  Day 6: from 12 midnight – 7 pm
  Day 7: from 12 midnight – 7 pm
- ✓ During the day, also pray

PRAYER POINTS

- ☐ You strongman administering my family ancestral altar, I bind you and destroy all your powers, be destroyed in the mighty name of Jesus Christ
- ☐ You ancestral altar, I command heaven to open and rain fire on you in the mighty name of Jesus Christ
- ☐ You family ancestral altar, you have no access to penetrate my life anymore in the mighty name of Jesus Christ
- ☐ I decree and declare that your arrows of wickedness can't affect me in the mighty name of Jesus Christ
- ☐ I command you ancestral altar, whatever belongs to me that you have been keeping, release it to me now……deliver it now, in the mighty name of Jesus Christ – Psalms 105:15

CONFESSION OF FAITH

I decree and declare that I brother/sister __________ on this ____ day of __________I was delivered from the ancestral altars and the Holy Spirit bears witness for my salvation and deliverance. In the name of the Father, the Son and The Holy Spirit I am free.

TESTIMONY: We overcome satan by the blood of the lamb and by the word of our testimony. Make sure that you testify to the glory of God and the shame of satan. Pray for your testimony that as you testify it touches others and deliver them. Satan has been using you to fulfil his evil desires now let God use for the expansion of His kingdom.

DELIVERANCE FROM CEMETERY ALTARS

A cemetery or graveyard is a place where dead people are buried. It is a place of death. It is a place of decay, desolation and being forsaken (Psalms 49:14; 88:5). It is a place of darkness, a place of defilement, corruption and pollution. The graveyard altar is an altar that swallows up its victims (Proverbs 1:12).

SYMPTOMS OF THE ATTACK OF THE CEMETERY ALTAR

- Dreams about the dead such as hearing their voices, eating or sleeping with them

- Getting married to dead persons in the dream
- Falling into pits in the dream and not able to come out
- Smell of death
- Having thoughts of suicide
- Dreaming coffins and graveyards
- Endless sicknesses and health problems
- Being hated by people
- Fear of death

INSTRUCTIONS

- ✓ Pray between 12 midnight to 0400 hrs. This is time to intensify prayer
- ✓ Fast and pray for five (5) days
  Day 1: from 12 midnight – 12 noon
  Day 2: from 12 midnight – 12 noon
  Day 3: from 12 midnight – 3 pm

Day 4: from 12 midnight – 6 pm
Day 5: from 12midnight – 12 midnight
✓ During the day, also pray

PRAYER POINTS

- ☐ You cemetery altars harassing my life, I release the sword of the Lord against you – Judges 7:18, in the mighty name of Jesus Christ.
- ☐ I release the sword of the Lord in your mouth and I declare that you will never open your mouth against me anymore – revelation 19:15, in the mighty name of Jesus Christ.
- ☐ I command angels with flaming swords to destroy you in the mighty name of Jesus.
- ☐ I command you cemetery altar to fall by the sword of the Lord – Psalms 63:10, in the mighty name of Jesus
- ☐ I break and destroy any soul tie with any dead person in Jesus mighty name.
- ☐ Every sickness released against me from the cemetery, die in the mighty name of Jesus Christ.
- ☐ Any ritual performed on the cemetery altar against my life, die in the mighty name of Jesus Christ.
- ☐ I destroy the association of witches and witchdoctors assigned against my life in the mighty name of Jesus Christ.
- ☐ Every satanic decree issued against my life is destroyed in the mighty name of Jesus Christ.
- ☐ I decree and declare that I am free from the bondage and influence of cemetery altars in the mighty name of Jesus Christ.

CONFESSION OF FAITH

I decree and declare that I brother/sister _______________on this _____ day of _______________ I was delivered from the cemetery altars and the Holy Spirit bears witness for my salvation and deliverance. In the name of the Father, the Son and The Holy Spirit I am free.

TESTIMONY: We overcome satan by the blood of the lamb and by the word of our testimony. Make sure that you testify to the glory of God and the shame of satan. Pray for your testimony that as you testify it touches others and deliver them. Satan has been using you to fulfil his evil desires now let God use for the expansion of His kingdom.

DELIVERANCE FROM WITCHCRAFT ALTARS

Numbers 23:23; Psalms 18:44-45; Luke 10:19; Matthew 3:10; Deuteronomy 18:10-12

The devil has a threefold ministry that is to steal, kill and to destroy. Witches are human beings that give their spirit and soul to the devil by entering into a covenant with him and because of that, the devil uses them as his agents to steal, kill and to destroy God's people. Their spirits and soul can easily move through the air. They use incarnations, invocations, manipulations, seduction, divination and enchantments to destroy their victims.

Witchcraft coven is an assembly or community of witches. It is a group of like-minded people who come together for evil purposes. Witchcraft involves communicating with demonic spirits impersonating the dead. The Bible clearly teaches that the dead cannot communicate with the living as there is a great charm that separates the dead from the living (Luke 16:26). God hates the practice of witchcraft. The penalty of practising witchcraft under Mosaic Law was death (Exodus 22:18; Leviticus 20:27; 1 Chronicles 10:13; Isaiah 8:19; Micah 5:12).

INSTRUCTIONS

- ✓ Pray between 12 midnight to 0400 hrs. This is time to intensify prayer
- ✓ Fast and pray for seven (7) days
  - Day 1: from 12 midnight – 12 noon
  - Day 2: from 12 midnight – 12 noon
  - Day 3: from 12 midnight – 3 pm
  - Day 4: from 12 midnight – 5 pm
  - Day 5: from 12 midnight – 7 pm
  - Day 6: from 12 midnight – 7 pm
  - Day 7: from 12 midnight – 7 pm
- ✓ During the day, also pray

PRAYER POINTS

- ❑ I destroy every witchcraft coven fighting against me at work, school, church, family be destroyed in the mighty name of Jesus.
- ❑ I destroy witchcraft horns exalted by witches, wizards and witchdoctors against my life in the mighty name of Jesus Christ.
- ❑ Every witchcraft power assigned to destroy my life catch fire and die in the mighty name of Jesus.
- ❑ I chop into pieces every witchcraft tongue-speaking against my life in the mighty name of Jesus.
- ❑ Every time witches come together for my destruction let thunder strike them in the mighty name of Jesus.

CONFESSION OF FAITH

I decree and declare that I brother/sister ______________ on this ____day of ______________ I was delivered from the witchcraft altars and the Holy Spirit bears witness for my salvation and deliverance. In the name of the Father, the Son and The Holy Spirit I am free.

TESTIMONY: We overcome satan by the blood of the lamb and by the word of our testimony. Make sure that you testify to the glory of God and the shame of satan. Pray for your testimony that as you testify it touches others and deliver them. Satan has been using you to fulfil his evil desires now let God use you for the expansion of His kingdom.

DELIVERANCE OF YOUR FAMILY

Praying for your family is part of Self-Deliverance. When your husband or your wife or children are bound by chains of satan, it means you are bound too because as a family you are one. Whatever happens to your husband or wife or children affects you directly. Self-Deliverance is not totally complete until you successfully pray for the deliverance of your family. Satan can use any member of the family to keep you in bondage. E.g. – you can suffer financially because of your husband or wife or your child. If any member of your family is attacked by sickness, it affects your finances, time or even your health. A child can make parents fight. So praying for the deliverance of your family is important.

Every day, as you pray for your family, believe that it will change, believe with all your heart, don't doubt, unto them that believe all things are possible. it does not matter how deep your husband/wife/children or child is into evil. The hand of the Lord is not short that it can't deliver. Don't give up, hold on and keep on praying. Wake up in the night and do midnight prayers. I assure you forces of darkness assigned to destroy your family will lose their grip on them, don't say I am tired. I know you have talked, parents, friends and pastors might have tried, but what talking couldn't do, the prayer of faith will do. Fight for your family, don't sit down there watching the devil destroying your marriage, no, no, no, you can't take no for yes. Do something. John 10:10; 1 Peter 5:8; James 4:7. satan is out there to destroy your family. Resist him through the power of prayer.

The most important thing you can do as a husband and wife is to confess your sins, repent and receive Jesus as your Lord and personal saviour (Romans 3:22-23). Marriage restoration is a process. May be your marriage has gone through marital hardships and challenges (Romans 12:12, 21; Psalms 51; Romans 12:9. Take everything to the Lord in prayer. Maybe your marriage is not going the way you had dreamed of. Believe in the power of God, how he can turn sadness into joy, despair into hope, chaos and confusion into peace.

God's Promise

Psalms 50:15, and call upon me in the day of trouble, and I will rescue you, and you will give me the glory'; 18:6 in my distress I called to the Lord; I cried to my Lord for help. From His temple He heard my voice; my cry came before Him, into His ears. Are you facing family troubles? From whatever angle they are coming from, cry out 'to the Lord, He will hear your voice and help you. Man, that is born of a woman is of few days and full of trouble (Job 14:1). Trust God for the deliverance of your family, cast all your cares and fears upon Him and He will deliver you. His promises unto His children are yes and amen. Bring your case to the Almighty God. He will avenge you. Be patient and persevere in prayer. The Lord will avenge you (Luke 18:1 – 8).

Pray for your family without ceasing. A man ought always to pray and not to faint. Remember the effectual, fervent prayer of a righteous man avails much (James 5:16). Many are the afflictions of the righteous but the Lord delivers him from all of them. Sorrow may endure in the night but joy comes in the morning. You must have the 'I can't give up" mentality.

If you want to know how to conduct family deliverance don't hesitate to contact us. Spiritual warfare or deliverance demands specific instructions from the Lord. When You call the man of God he will help you to do Family Spiritual Mapping and give you prophetic instructions for the deliverance of your family.

PRAYING FOR YOUR WIFE-A praying husband

1 Peter 3:7, part of dwelling with your wife with understanding means recognising that your wife is in need of your covering, protection and love. You need to honour her in your thoughts, action and words. If you don't, your prayers are hindered. One of the best ways to honour your wife is to pray for her from a heart that is clean before God. Praying for your wife must begin with you praying for yourself. Satan does not want your marriage to succeed. He will come up with plans and strategies to destroy it. But you're as the head of the family, Jesus has given you the power to stop him through your prayers.

Mathew 12:25. It is a horrible thing to have strife in your marriage. It will make your marriage miserable. And this will affect every area of your life. When all these begin to happen then it means your house is divided. Jesus said, 'every kingdom divided against itself will not stand"

A praying husband is a godly husband. To be godly means you have God, it means the spirit of God lives in you (Galatians 2:20; Titus 2:12).

Below is a list of some of the things you should not forget when praying for your wife;

- Her Christian life. Pray for her relationship with God
- Her marriage. Pray that love will continue to grow between you and your wife.
- Her ministry in the work of God

- ☐ Her motherhood
- ☐ Her emotions and moods
- ☐ Her submission and obedience
- ☐ Her beauty
- ☐ Her sexuality
- ☐ Her work

PRAYER POINTS

- ☐ Father God, I am so thankful for my wife. Thank you for her life. Thank you, Lord, for her love for me. Thank you for every detail about her that makes her so unique.
- ☐ Father, I pray that my wife and I would be of value to each other valued. Help us to love each other
- ☐ I pray that I and my wife would work together to build your kingdom and to fulfil your will
- ☐ Lord, bless my marriage. Make your face to shine upon me and my wife, and be gracious unto us (Numbers 6:24-26)
- ☐ Father God! In blessing, bless us, and in multiplying, multiply us as the stars of heaven and as the sand of the seashore.
- ☐ Father, God! Let your arm be revealed in my marriage (Isaiah 40:5)
- ☐ I release the fire of God to consume every spell, curses and every witchcraft assigned to destroy my marriage (Deut 7:5)
- ☐ Every satanic power sent to destroy my wife catch fire and die, be destroyed in the mighty name of Jesus.
- ☐ I release Gods hot thunderbolt against anti-marriage altar, be destroyed in the mighty name of Jesus, I decree and declare you can't destroy my wife (Psalms 78:48)
- ☐ I release the fire of the presence of God in my marriage in the mighty name of Jesus.
- ☐ I decree and declare that my marriage is redeemed from the curse of the law (Gal 3:13), therefore every marital curse from my father's side, my mother's side and from my in-law's side do not affect my marriage in the mighty name of Jesus.
- ☐ I decree and declare that I and my wife____________ are of one mind, that we walk in unity and there is no division among us. I confess that we are perfectly joined together,

we walk in agreement and we have the same Spirit of God inside of us

☐ I decree and declare that I and my wife ___________________ love each other so much. Our love is solidified in the faith and it is that same love that we share for one another that covers a multitude of faults and mistakes between us

☐ I decree and declare that there is no bitterness and strife between me and my wife, neither is there any anger, fighting, evil speaking or malice towards each other

☐ I am my wife's biggest encourager. The words that I speak daily to my wife are words that will build her up and never to tear her down.

☐ I and my wife are kind towards each other, we are tender-hearted towards one another, and we forgive one another, just as God has forgiven us through His son Jesus Christ

☐ I decree and declare that no weapon fashioned against our marriage shall be able to prosper against us in any way. Every word spoken against my marriage shall fall to the ground and die

☐ I decree and declare that neither I nor my wife shall accept or receive any thought of the devil, thoughts of unfaithfulness, separation or divorce. We will only take the thoughts of God, thoughts of peace, joy, gentleness, goodness and meekness

☐ Father, God! Give the necks of enemies of my family so that I may destroy them that hate my family (Psalm 18:40)

☐ I decree and declare that it is God who has joined us together in marriage, therefore no person, spirit, force or power, no mistake committed by me or my wife, no fault shall be able to separate us in the mighty name of Jesus.

Note – You wife can also pray the above prayer. You can print this prophetic decree and carry it wherever you go and always make decrees. The Lord says "You shall decree a thing and it shall establish it for you"

PRAYING FOR YOUR HUSBAND - A Praying Wife

Praying for your husband is putting God in the centre of your marriage.it is your responsibility as a wife to pray for your husband. Your husband needs your prayers. He is the most important person in your life, therefore you can't afford not to pray for him. This is someone you are going to spend the rest of your life with. Do you want your husband to be all that God called him to be? The most powerful thing that you can do for him is to pray for him daily.

Every day your husband faces temptations, attacks, setbacks and challenges that test his commitment to God. As his wife, it is your responsibility to continually pray for him. Ask the Holy Spirit to direct you as you pray for your husband so that you could pray about the real issues he is facing. Imagine what would happen if wives made it a habit to pray for their husbands, how your marriage and family would look like. How can you, as a wife make the greatest impact on the life of your husband? You can do it by earnestly, regularly and passionately praying for him.it has been said "behind every great man there is a great woman.

A godly praying wife is one of the greatest blessings a man can receive in his life. A praying wife is like a rare jewel. She is like a scarce commodity. A godly wife is a gift from God to her husband. She is the source of great joy to her husband. Job 2:9-10, Job's wife did not seem to be a godly virtuous woman. She did not fear God and she spoke like a fool. A foolish woman builds her house and thereafter destroys it whereas a Godly wife is a good woman. She helps her husband (Ecc 4:9-10). she trusts God and she serves Him faithfully. She brings honour to her husband. She is a crown to her husband (Proverbs 12:4) her price is far above rubies (Proverbs 31:10) she is praised by her family and by all that know her (Proverbs 31:30-31), the heart of her husband safely trusts in her, she labours diligently from morning to night for her household, she is a woman of wisdom, honour and strength, her children call her blessed. I want you to know as a wife that you have the power to build up your husband or to tear him down.

PRAYER POINTS

- ☐   Lord, I pray that you would convict my husband, Mr ______________ of any error in his life. Let nothing be covered that will not be known (Mathew 10:26)
- ☐   Cleanse him from any secret sins and teach him to be a person who is quick to confess when he is wrong (Psalms

19:12), bring him into full repentance before you.

☐ Take away all pride that would cause him to deny his faults and work into his soul, let him have the humility of heart so that he will receive the honour You have for him (Proverbs 15:33)

☐ Father, you said I will call upon you in the day of trouble and you will deliver me (Psalms 50:12). I call upon you now and ask that you would work deliverance in my husband's life. Deliver him from anything that is binding and holding him captive. Set him free from (e.g. adultery) ______________, deliver him quickly oh, Lord.

☐ Father, please lift up my husband Mr__________________ from the hands of satan (Psalms 31:2, 15)

☐ Father, God! Keep my husband from discouragement and help him to be confident that you have begun a good work in him and you will complete it (Philippians 1:6). Give, my husband Mr_________________ the certainty that even in his most hopeless state, when he finds it impossible to change, You Lord can change everything in his life

☐ I pray you, my husband Mr______________ that your eyes be opened so that you may come to a place of understanding where you can recognize the work of satan and cry out to God for your help

☐ I pray for you, my husband that you may be strong in the Lord and put on the whole armour of God so you can stand against the wiles of the devil in the evil day. (Ephesians 6:12-18)

☐ I take authority over every evil power sent to destroy my husband in the mighty name of Jesus

☐ I decree and declare that you my husband______________, you a great husband, and you are my man, you are a gift from God. _________________, my husband, you always make me feel loved, you are God sent into my life, you make me feel that I am a great woman. My husband, _____________________ you are so smart, you are amazing, you are wonderfully made, you are unique, you are a strong man, you are a hard worker.

☐ My husband _____________, you are a great lover. When

you hold me tight I feel safe in your hands. I will always be by your side; I am yours forever. I am blessed you are my husband. You are a godly man. Thank you for leading our family in a godly way, being your wife is a great honour indeed. I love how steady and stable you are; it makes me feel secure.

- Our children are blessed you are their father. I am a better woman because you are my husband. I have learnt so much from you. You are my favourite person in the entire world. You are a rock. I am proud to be your wife. I totally trust you. You always inspire me to be the best I can. You are my dream come true. I will always be loyal to you. No other man could even come close. I will always honour you. You will always have my heart.

- Thank you for being a faithful husband. You have a lot to offer. You have helped me to become a better woman. You are a godly man. I love it when you teach me the word of God. I love just being with you. I will love you always and forever.

Note – You husband can also pray the above prayer. You can print this prophetic decree and carry it wherever you go and always make decrees. The Lord says "You shall decree a thing and I shall establish it for you".

PRAYING FOR YOUR CHILD/CHILDREN

2 Timothy 1:5, Timothy was raised by a godly grandmother named Lois and a godly mother named Eunice. Their influence leads to his salvation. Acts 16:2, people spoke well of him because of the influence he got from his mother and grandmother.

PRAYER POINTS

- Father God, I ask you to surround my children with your blessings and favour, may you shine your face on them (Psalms 90:17)

- I pray that my children would grow in the fruit of the spirit and that godly character qualities be evident in their lives (Galatians 5:22-23)

- I decree that no weapon fashioned against my children shall prosper, and that God is their constant shield and defender, that He would hide them in His presence (Psalms 91:1-4)

☐ Father God, I ask you to surround my children with godly people, guard them against negative people, destiny killers and useless people (1 Corinthians 15:33)

☐ Father, I ask you to give my children wisdom and direction in making decisions (Prov 3:5; Psalms 37:1 -6; James 1:5)

☐ Father help my children to live in holiness and purity (1 Peter 1:15-16)

☐ I take authority over every spirit assigned to destroy the lives of my children, I know satan is a thief, killer and destroyer (John 10:10), be destroyed in the mighty name of Jesus

☐ I decree and declare that my failures will not be my children's failure, what stopped me in life can't stop my children in the mighty name of Jesus

☐ I decree and declare that my children will excel in everything they do, they shall be like a watered garden in the mighty name of Jesus

☐ I decree and declare that my children are free from generational curses and all satanic family altars in the mighty name of Jesus

☐ I pray for you my son/daughter ______________believe in the Lord Jesus, and you will saved(Acts 16:31), the Lord bless you and keep you, the Lord make His face to shine on you and be gracious to you, the Lord turn His face toward you and give you peace (Numbers 6:24-26), be strong and courageous, Do not be afraid of life, face life fearlessly, always be courageous, when you face life challenges lean on the Lord, for the Lord your God will be with you wherever you go (Joshua 1:9). Only fear the Lord and serve Him faithfully with all your heart (1 Samuel 12:24).

☐ I decree and declare that your life is blessed in the mighty name of Jesus.

DELIVERANCE FROM SPIRIT OF REJECTION

Rejection is an anti – Christ spirit. This spirit makes people not to accept you, not to welcome you, not to value you. It opposes the image of God in a person's life. The purpose of the spirit of rejection is to make you feel useless and rejected and unwanted.

The root of rejection is misplaced identity. Don't base your identity on the negative things that people say about you. Base your identity on what and who God says you are. Don't allow satan and his children to define who you are. David was rejected and treated as a shepherd boy and yet he was a king. They called him a shepherd boy but that was not his real identity. He was born to be king in Israel. God took advantage of the situation, He used it to train and prepare him for battles that lied ahead of him. He was the least recognised among his brothers, yet he was favoured by God. It is your turn to be favoured. All things work together for good unto them that are called according to His purpose. Whatever satan might have used to attack your identity, use it to grow stronger and to become better in Christ Jesus. Having done all be strong in the   Lord and in the power of His might - Ephesians 1:3-6; 2:8-9; 6:10.

You must deal with rejection head-on. All negative emotions birthed by rejection such as feelings of sadness, disappointment, embarrassment and discouragement, face them. Don't run away. Sometimes you must expect rejection, Jesus was rejected of men (Isaiah 53:3). Don't be afraid to face rejection.

As you deal with the spirit of rejection you should also be delivered from Self-Rejection. This is whereby a person rejects himself. They do not like who they are. Self-Rejection leads to Self-hate and Self-Unforgiveness. Don't hate yourself because you made mistakes in the past which you deeply regret.

Spirit of rejection is a wicked anti-Christ spirit. It wants to wound you deeply by;

Attacking the very person that you are

Destroying your self – esteem

Attacking your purpose of life

Hindering you to become all that God wants you to become

People who faced rejection and abuse when they were young grow up with unresolved emotional wounds and if these wounds are not dealt with, they cause spiritual wounds such as unforgiveness, jealousy, hatred and they can even be tempted to blame God for the things they suffered

Common Symptoms of rejection

- ☐ Rebellion
- ☐ Misplaced identity
- ☐ The tendency to reject others
- ☐ The need to be accepted
- ☐ Self- pity
- ☐ A sense of pride
- ☐ The need to always be right
- ☐ Feelings of insecurity or hopelessness
- ☐ Hard to receive correction
- ☐ Stubbornness

Prayer Points

- ☐ I lose myself from the bond of rejection in the mighty name of Jesus – Luke 13:16
- ☐ I command all spirits controlling my life, rooted in rejection to come out in the mighty name of Jesus
- ☐ I release Holy Ghost fire to destroy all fetters and shackles of rejection, be destroyed in the mighty name of Jesus
- ☐ I command you spirit to come out of my life in the mighty name of Jesus
- ☐ Thank you, Father, for delivering me.

The key to overcoming rejection is to solve the identity problem. Know who you are in Christ Jesus.

DELIVERANCE FROM ANGER

Proverbs 16:32; Romans 1:18-32; Galatians 5:16-26

Anger destroys lives. It eats away like a gnawing canker and divides families, friends and loved ones; it also destroys self. Anger may be directed towards a wife, husband, taxi man, a church member, the preacher, or family members and loved ones, but regardless of who our anger is directed towards, we need to remember: "anger resteth in the bosom of fools".

One who masters self and the lusts of the heart is greater than mighty conquerors for "He that is slow to anger is better than the mighty; and he that ruleth his spirit than he that taketh a city ", -Prov 16:32. This is a spiritual battle in which "we draw nigh unto God and find rest unto our souls".

Anger is a very deadly and destructive force. To learn to avoid wrath is a great blessing for "He that is slow to wrath is of great understanding: but he that is hasty of spirit exalteth folly "–Prov 14:29. When one is slow to wrath they understand not only self but also the principles that God has given us to deal with anger; they are of great "understanding. But when one is not slow to wrath, they exalt folly.

How we respond when anger is directed towards us matters a lot and has to do with avoiding anger for "A soft answer turneth away wrath: but grievous words stir up anger "- Prov 15:1. "Grievous words "stir up a volatile mixture of anger and wrath. The cup is poison! Grievous words are like pouring petrol on fire: it gets bigger and hotter. But a "soft answer" is like pouring water on the fire; it quenches the fire.

Anger causes suffering. Anger can cause us to suffer both mentally and physically. Anger affects our health for "A man of great wrath shall suffer punishment "- Prov 19:19. Not only does God punish for the sin of anger but a person given to anger actually punishes themselves.

Paul knew this and wrote "Be ye angry, and sin not: let not the sun go down upon your wrath: neither give place to the devil "Eph 4:26-27. If anger is not dealt with daily and it is carried over into the next day, it wears us down. Carrying anger around, day after day is giving "a place to the devil. "The devil likes nothing better than to separate loved ones and destroy lives. We must remember: when we carry anger around day after day we are giving the devil a place in our life; we have become his captive –Prov 19:19. "A man of great wrath shall suffer punishment: for if thou deliver him, yet thou must do it again ". A man of great wrath ", is a person that is angry over and over again. If you help them out of one angry bout "thou must do it again", that is why psychoanalyzing anger will not cure the problem. Anger must be properly observed as sin for "an angry man aboundeth in transgression "-Prov 29:22… Anger is probably one of the most deadly forces we deal with daily.

Much anger is a result of not accepting particular circumstances in life.

People may believe that their anger is hurting the person they are angry at but they are actually destroying themselves. "But I say unto you, love your enemies, bless them that curse you, do good to them that hate you, and pray for them which despitefully use you, and persecute you"-Matthew 5:44. Jesus has taught us, to do well to those who despitefully use us and pray for them. If they are in such error, let's be honest about it and pray for their souls that God may turn them around that they might please Jesus Christ in their lives. How difficult or almost it is too impossible to pray for a person and stay mad at them for very long.

Anger has many children and they are all vicious. Paul mentions them time and again in his epistles as he instructs us to "put off all these; anger, wrath, malice, blasphemy, filthy communication out of your mouth "-Col 3:8. As we read these words we should be careful to notice the sinful progression that anger leads us into; anger first; then wrath; then malice; then blasphemy which opens up to filthy communication of the mouth. This is the exact pattern Haman followed as he plotted the death of Mordecai.

PRAYER

Pray and ask God to forgive you for having allowed satan to control you with the spirit of anger. After you have confessed all your sins regarding anger, conduct self-deliverance. Command anger to come out of your life.

Forgive those who wronged you, and also ask God to forgive you for hurting His people with your anger.

After you have prayed 'believe that you are free, totally delivered. Start to make peace with others' 'blessed are the peacemakers for theirs is the kingdom of God…follow peace with all men"

SELF ESTABLISHMENT

1. Repent and forsake all your sins (1 John 1:9).
    (Lust, fornication, adultery, gossiping, unforgiveness, bitterness, anger, jealousy etc.).
2. Ask God to thoroughly purge and cleanse you by the precious blood of Jesus Christ
    (Hebrews 9:22)
3. Take time to praise and worship God (Ps 100:4).
4. Pray for holiness and the fear of God in your life (Ps 15; Hebrews 12:14; Ps 51)
5. Wait in God's presence, be still and know that He is God. Let God talk to you and give you insight, feel and experience His power, anointing and His transforming glory.
6. Feel the presence of the Son and of the Holy Spirit.
7. Picturize and meditate deeply, see the hand of God changing you, delivering you from the power of sin.
8. See and feel the fire of the Holy Ghost refining you, see the Lord.
9. Continue to pray and tell God how much you are hungry for Him; how much you are thirsty for Him.
10. Tell God you are coming to Him and you don't want to look back any more. Ask for grace and mercy to be true to God.
11. Acknowledge God as the source of life, power and strength. Praise and worship Him.
12. Pray in the spirit.
13. Make warfare against satan, fight for your life-Matthew 11:12, put on the whole armour of God. Use spiritual weapons to fight (the blood, the word, Holy Ghost Fire etc.)
14. Deal with satanic altars, foundations and gates fighting against your life.

CHAPTER 5
PRAYER ALTAR

HOW TO BUILD AN ALTAR UNTO THE LORD

Only a person who is spiritually alive and qualified can raise an altar. When God begins to speak to people about altars, He wants to enter into a fresh covenant with them. He wants to visit the land. He wants to bring about changes. That is why we keep the altars of our soul alive.

Building an altar unto the Lord will cost you something. Before you can experience the manifestation of God and His fire in your life, family, ministry and church there is a need to repair and rebuild the altar of God in your life. The fire and power we receive from Him are determined by our level of commitment, consecration and separation unto Him. We need total consecration by separating ourselves from ungodliness, compromise and worldliness then repent and recommit ourselves to God.

REQUIREMENTS

- ☐ Salvation –you must be born again (Genesis 24:3-4).
- ☐ Destroy the old altar and replace it with a new altar (Judges 6:22-35).
- ☐ Passion –you must have a hunger for God (1 Kings 5:5).
- ☐ Faith in God (Hebrews 11:6).
- ☐ Die to self (Galatians 2:20).
- ☐ Set your priorities in order (Matthew 6:21).
- ☐ You must have a plan
- ☐ Be altar conscious

HOW TO RAISE AN ALTAR

1. Locate a spot and make it a place of worship and consecration.

2. Hallow it by pouring anointing oil on it.

3. Call upon the name of the Lord and ask the three to bear record on earth and in heaven to take note that you are raising an altar to Him on that spot.

4. Name the altar e.g. an altar of consecration, an altar of remembrance, an altar of righteousness, an altar of restoration, an altar of mercy etc.

5. Mark your altar. God directed Israel to use twelve stones to raise Israel's national altar.

You have to mark your altar with something memorable.

6. Declare the intention, aim or purpose of the altar you have built.

PERSONAL ALTAR

To build a personal altar simply means setting time aside to meet God one-on-one. It comes with a specific time at which you seek the face of God through worship, praises, thanksgiving and prayer. It means offering yourself as a living sacrifice, holy and acceptable unto God. Sacrifice means giving up the things that you value most in your life to God to express the sincerity of your heart to Him so that you may obtain His favour, it means giving up something valuable or important to somebody. It is something that is given away, which is usually painful to let go. Sacrifice is never convenient. Sacrifices are such offerings that are never convenient to the giver.

They are given out for the purpose of receiving answers, results and favour from God. It is the sacrifice that empowers the altar. Without the sacrifice the altar is powerless. If you present your body as a living sacrifice unto Him, you will be rooted in him and will flourish like the palm tree because if you are rooted in Him you get nourishment from Him. And if you get nourishment from him you will be His reflection.

This is how Christ is formed in us (Psalms 92:12; John 15:1-8). There is no how you can abide in Him without building a personal altar. An altar is a place of spiritual transaction. It is a place of slaughter. It is a place of destiny exchange where man either encounters God or the devil. Altars are backed up and equipped with the power and influence of spoken words. Majority of our problems are a result of words spoken by someone on the evil altar.

You have to build an altar for the Lord in your heart. Maintain it, and visit it frequently. This is where you take your sins, sorrows, faults and failures to God. It is at the altar where you experience God as a consuming fire. You will never experience Him as the God who answers by fire in your personal life until you build an altar in your heart for Him. Remember that your body is the temple of the Holy Spirit (1 Corinthians 6:12; 2 Corinthians 6:16; 1 Peter 2:5; 1 Chronicles 21:26).

Your speed and successes in life are determined by the power of your altar and the power of your altar is determined by your consecration. If your godly altar is destroyed, you will be a victim of satanic altars. Personal altar means 'Quite Time' your time alone with God.

A CALL TO REPAIR YOUR PERSONAL ALTAR

God is calling us to repair and rebuild destroyed and neglected altars of our lives. God eagerly desires to spend time with you. Daniel built an altar of prayer. He prayed three times a day (Daniel 6: 10- 11). He prayed, thanked God and made supplication before him.

1. Repent- Remember therefore from whence thou art fallen and repent and do the first works (Revelation 2:5; 2 Chronicles 7:14). Admit the fact that you have backslidden. You know what caused you to backslide.
2. Surrender all to Jesus Christ. He is willing to deliver you from all sins that you have been battling with. Don't give up. Come to Him by faith and He will help you.
3. Rededicate everything about yourself to Christ and He will release fresh fire upon you. Keep the fire on the altar burning (Leviticus 6:13).
4. Commitment- commit yourself to please God in everything you do. We must love each other. God's fire cannot continue burning where there is no love. Our love must be practical. If we want the fire of God to continue burning in our lives, families and church we must practice love. The reason why sometimes we pray but we don't see revival is because of

lack of love (Acts 4:33-37; 2:45-47).

5. Consecration- In order to keep the fire burning you must live a life of consecration. This means giving your life continually to prayer and the ministry of the word (Acts 6:4).

6. Separation- Keep away from sin and the cares of this world (1 Samuel 7:3-4).

FAMILY ALTAR

This is a specific time set aside by the family to come together to study the word of God, praise and worship God together. Satan hates family altars. He knows that a family that prays together stays together. Many have destroyed their family altars. No matter how busy we are, we must not allow anything to take the place of the family altar.

The family altar is where we go to worship God, thank and praise Him. This is where we come to present our family affairs to Him. When the family altar gets destroyed, satan builds his altar and the altar that he builds determines what happens in the family.

The atmosphere of the family will be influenced by satanic powers, then you will begin to experience misuse of money, children becoming rebellious, satanic dreams, the joy of the Lord will no longer be your portion, unnecessary disputes, late going to church, rebellion against church leadership, not paying tithes and many evil will befall the family.

PRAYING FOR YOUR ALTAR

Every satanic altar fighting against my Personal altar and Family altar, I come against you in the name of the resurrected Jesus, whose I am and whom I serve, I command you to bow and confess that my altars are superior to you because the Lion of the Tribe of Judah, the Son of the living God, He who has the key of the house of David, reigns upon my altar in the mighty name of Jesus Christ

I establish divine parameters, boundaries and borders, and legislate and establish the laws of the kingdom of heaven to govern all my altars in the mighty name of Jesus Christ.

PRAYERS

1. PRAYERS FOR STUDENTS

A school is an important place because it is where you receive an education. It has been said, knowledge is power. Enjoying school then is important as enjoying it will allow you to feel good each day about attending school classes and will help you to focus and enjoy learning the things you are learning. As a student, you must have school loving Mind-Set.

PRAYER POINTS

- ☐ Father God, you the creator of all things, you are the true source of light, knowledge, wisdom and understanding. Give me clear understanding, a retentive memory and the ability to grasp everything correctly when I am been taught and give me the ability to express myself in the mighty name of Jesus

- ☐ Father, God! Help me to keep learning every day of my life, no matter what the subject may be, help me to stay focused on my educational studies in the mighty name of Jesus.

- ☐ Holy Spirit of the living God, encourage me when the studies are difficult, when I am tempted to give up and when my brain is slow to learn in the mighty name of Jesus.

- ☐ Give me the grace to put my knowledge to use in the mighty name of Jesus.

- ☐ Father God, by the covering of the blood of Jesus, I ask you to guard my heart and my mind against academic witchcraft in the mighty name of Jesus.

- ☐ Father, I ask you to give me great enthusiasm for my studies. May you inspire me each and every day, may each class bring fresh inspiration to my school work in the mighty name of Jesus

- ☐ I bind and cast out every spirit assigned to attack and harass me academically in the mighty name of Jesus

- ☐ I cast out every spirit of academic failure in the mighty name of Jesus

- ☐ I pray for wisdom upon all my teachers in the mighty name of Jesus

☐ I declare the blessings of the Lord upon my fellow students and I pray for their salvation that they may know Jesus Christ as their Lord and personal saviour.

A PRAYER BEFORE A TEST

Lord Jesus, I pray that you guide me as I take this test, so that I may do my best. Open my mind, clear my thoughts, relax my mind and body and grant me perfect concentration so that I may use the knowledge I have gained to pass this test. Holy Spirit of God, remind me everything that I have to remember as I take this test, the word of God says that when you have come you will remind me all things. In the mighty name of Jesus!

PROPHETIC DECREES

When you pray this prayer, visualize and pray by faith. See the thing you are declaring happening. Feel the anointing of the Holy Spirit destroying academic jokes. E.g. – I enjoy attending class each day (see yourself in class, see your teacher, classmates etc., do it by faith in the name of Jesus), I always participate in class (see yourself in class, visualize your teacher asking a question, see yourself raising your hand to answer the question, see yourself asking questions in class etc.)

☐ I enjoy attending class each day.
☐ I find it easy to stay focused in class.
☐ I always make sure I get all my homework done on time, I love and enjoy doing my homework.
☐ I am extremely focused on passing all my subjects, I love studying.
☐ I am always participating in class.
☐ I never sleep in class – I am always energetic and attentive.
☐ I am successful academically.
☐ I am organised, hardworking creative and smart
☐ I will complete standard/form_________- successfully and easily
☐ I pass my exams easily
☐ I am a great student
☐ Success is my due reward
☐ I make all A's

- ☐ My school is wonderful and my teachers are marvellous and my classmates are terrific
- ☐ Studying comes easily and I enjoy studying
- ☐ I have perfect memory and I can recall with ease
- ☐ My memory is sharp
- ☐ I always remember everything that I learn
- ☐ I concentrate easily and I am immune to distraction
- ☐ I realise that this is the age to study and prepare for the future and I am doing so sincerely
- ☐ I understand that habits make a pattern and I develop good habits
- ☐ I can be whatever I want to be
- ☐ I know that friends and friendship make a huge impact in life and hence I am careful in choosing my friends.

2. PRAYERS FOR BUSINESS

Father, God! Thank you for the opportunity to run this business. I trust in your wisdom as I seek to work hard to make it secure and prosperous. I confess that my business is nothing without you and therefore my trust concerning this business is completely in you, in the mighty name of Jesus.

REPENTANCE

I repent and receive forgiveness for all sins that I have and I might have committed that can hinder my business to prosper and to attract customers and hence attract wealth and abundance in my life (Ephesians 4:27; 1 John 1:9).

RESTORATION

- ☐ Father, God! I pray for every financial hedge that has been destroyed in my life to be restored (Exodus 10:38)
- ☐ Father, God! Turn every anti – prosperity curse that enemies of my business can try to release against my business into a blessing – Nehemiah 13:2
- ☐ I ask for your guidance as I build and shape this business

CLEANSING YOUR BUSINESS (THE BUILDING AND GROUND)

- ☐ Father, God! As I use this Salt-Water remedy/anointing oil/anointed water I decree and declare that this ___________________is cleansed from all anti-business evil spirits.
- ☐ I destroy all assignments of satan against my business and I decree that enemies of my business will come in one way and be scattered in seven different directions – Deuteronomy 28:7
- ☐ I decree a casting down of all spirits of mammon, cankerworms, palmerworm, caterpillar and locust that are assigned by satan to eat my business

PROPHETIC DECREES OVER THE BUSINESS - Do this prayer for seven consecutive days.

- ☐ I decree that when other business people are chasing for customers I will have surplus
- ☐ I decree that favour will come to my business from everywhere, henceforth the favour of God will overrun me and make a way for me in every area of my business
- ☐ I command the release of all my expectations in my business
- ☐ I decree that my business will flourish like a palm tree and grow like a cider in Lebanon – Psalms 92:12, and it shall be like a tree that is planted by the riverside – Jeremiah 17:7-8 and that it shall ever be green like a watered garden and ever be flowing with customers like a spring of water, whose waters never fail.
- ☐ I decree and declare that from today my business will prosper and continue to prosper until it is prosperous (Genesis 26:13)
- ☐ I promise God that I will be faithful in business and will be a faithful tither and hence no devourer will come near my business (Malachi 3:10).

Take a seed of any amount of money you may feel lead by the Holy Spirit to give. Lay it on your Altar as a sacrifice to unlock all your financial doors.

For seven consecutive days, when you pray to lift up the sacrifice before God and decree by faith in the name of Jesus Christ that all your financial doors are opened. At the end of the seven days

go and sow your seed to your man of God

If you want to know how to conduct business deliverance and how to build a Business Altar don't hesitate to contact us. Spiritual warfare or deliverance demands specific instructions from the Lord. When You call the man of God he will help you to do Business Spiritual Mapping and give you prophetic instructions for the deliverance of your business and teach you how to erect a Business Altar.

3. PRAYERS TO OVERCOME EVIL PEOPLE IN THE WORKPLACE

Satan has strategically placed his children where you are working to ensure that he destroys your life. As a child of God, you need to be able to discern. Some of these witches in the workplace are not easy to identify them. You focus on the wrong people thinking that they are the source of your troubles in the workplace while the witch behind all your troubles is in a corner somewhere just watching. It is possible that they can act nice towards you while you are their assignment.

Children of satan are tricky like their father satan. John 8:44'they are of their father the devil, and the lust of their father they will do...." Be wise

Are you facing witchcraft and satanic attacks where you are working? Fear not for the Lord your God is with you, be not dismayed, He is with you, he will strengthen you, and all that are incensed against you shall be ashamed and confounded, they shall be as nothing and they that strive with you shall perish, you will look for them but not find them and they that war against you shall be as nothing (Isaiah 41:10-12). It does not matter the satanic powers they are using; you are covered by the blood of Jesus.

Signs of Witchcraft in the Work Place

1. An oppressive environment

This whereby satan uses his children to oppress you. The work environment becomes oppressive in such a way that when you get to work you feel the burden, in meetings you are not free to comment, they always attack you and there is always tension. They deliberately do all this to restrain your ability and to hinder you to reach your full potential and at the end, you lose hope.

2. Lies and false accusations

They will create stories against you and gossip you. They will give a false account against you either written or verbal to damage and destroy you. By so doing they want to destroy your professional reputation. Your boss will be calling you every day to tell you all the negatives.

3. Anger

When you realise that most people are always angry with you in the workplace, whereby it's like you are a problem to people, just know you are under a witchcraft attack.

4. Hatred and Rejection

Everybody will want to keep away from you. Every time you hear about meetings late and they will say they told you. When you are appointed to attend meetings or workshops they hide everything from you. Instead of recommending you they disapprove and condemn you. Witchcraft!

5. Continual fatigue

Are you always tired at work? You have lost motivation and the desire to work is dying every day. This is the work of witchcraft in the workplace. Satan wants to bring you weariness so that you give up and quit.

6. Forgetfulness

If you are fond of forgetting to do your work. You forget there is a meeting, you forget to submit whatever you were supposed to submit, etc. They are bewitching you.

7. Failing to reach targets

That's why you must be delivered from procrastination. Satan is using the spirit of procrastination to attack, he wants to make you useless.

8. Always late at work

No matter how much you try, you are always late. Late coming is a demon.

PRAYER POINTS

- ☐ Father God, I thank you for blessing me and giving a place to work in. I am grateful for all the good things you continue to do for me be thou glorified in the mighty name of Jesus.
- ☐ Father God, arise and let the destructive plans of my enemies at work be scattered in the mighty name of Jesus.
- ☐ Father God! Hide me from Mr/Mrs/Ms_____________ who is planning to destroy my job and my position in the mighty name of Jesus.
- ☐ Every door of oppression opened against me at my workplace, be closed in the mighty name of Jesus.
- ☐ Every witchcraft coven working against my life at my workplace, be exposed in the mighty name of Jesus.
- ☐ Those planning to destroy me at my workplace, you shall not succeed, especially you Mr/Mrs/Ms___________ in the mighty name of Jesus.
- ☐ I resist and reject every evil report concerning my job in the mighty name of Jesus.
- ☐ My father, reveal to me anyone that does not want me to be promoted at my workplace, arrest and disgrace such person in the mighty name of Jesus.
- ☐ Any power using any of my bosses or my colleagues to attack me, your expiry date has come, expire in the mighty name of Jesus.
- ☐ Let every person at my workplace who has been taking my name to witchcraft covens, sangomas or witchdoctors to destroy my life repent and stop it, I command you to stop, if you refuse to stop, receive thunder, in the mighty name of Jesus. You can't escape tonight, no hiding place in the mighty name of Jesus….be tormented, receive the same destruction you meant for me in the mighty name of Jesus.
- ☐ I decree and declare that those who have been fighting against me in the workplace from today they shall bow down to me with their faces towards the earth and lick up the dust

of my feet (mention their names and command them to bow down to you) – Isaiah 49:23.

☐ Mr/Mrs/Ms ________________ from today when you see me you will bend unto me, you will bow yourself down at the sole of my feet and you shall call me the blessed of the Lord (Isaiah 60:14).

☐ I decree and declare that like a serpent you will lick the dust off my feet and every time you see me you shall be like a worm and you shall be afraid because of me (Micah 7:17).

☐ You shall see it and shame shall cover you and you shall be trodden down like the mire of the streets (Micah 7:10).

☐ I decree and declare that all of you who rejoiced at my hurt shall be brought to confusion and shall be clothed with shame and dishonour (Psalms 35:26)

☐ Father, God! I thank You, You are the God who prepares a table for me in front of my enemies. You are the God who crowns my mouth with good things. My tears will not be my meat anymore, surely goodness and mercy shall follow me all the days of my life (Psalm 23:5,6;42:3)

4. PRAYERS FOR DELIVERANCE, HEALING AND GOOD HEALTH

Are you facing a difficult disease or illness? You can cry out to God for healing, cry out to Him by faith in the name of Jesus and receive your healing. Do you feel scared and unsure of the future because of what the Doctor said? God wants to heal you.

☐ Father, God! You are Jehovah – Rapha, the God who heals. I come to you for divine healing. I absolutely believe you have the power to heal. Father, I need your healing and grace. Root out sickness and disease out of my body. And father, restore me to full health in mind and body in the mighty name of Jesus

☐ Let your healing power touch me and bring me total healing (Luke 9:6) in the mighty name of Jesus.

☐ I release the fire of the Holy Ghost to burn out sickness and disease operating in my life in the mighty name of Jesus

☐ I decree and declare that no sickness or disease will come near my dwelling (Psalms 91:10) in the mighty name of

Jesus

☐ I decree and declare that I am healed (Isaiah 53:5) in the mighty name of Jesus

5. PRAYERS TO DESTROY MARINE ALTARS

RELEASE THE FIRE OF GOD

☐ A fire goes before you, O Lord, and burns up your enemies (Ps 97:3).

☐ Marine altars I release the fire of God over you, be burned.

☐ I release the fire of God to burn the idols, mirrors and all satanic objects and tools of marine altars (Deuteronomy 7:5).

☐ I release the fire of God to burn wicked spirits of marine powers (Ps 106:18).

RELEASE THE POWER OF THE BLOOD

☐ I sprinkle the blood of Jesus Christ over my life and I receive divine protection, multiplied by grace and peace (1 Peter 1:2).

☐ I break the power of sin and iniquity in my life through the blood of Jesus
(Hebrews 10:17)

☐ Marine altars, powers and spirits, I overcome you through the blood of Jesus (Revelation 12:1)

6. PRAYERS TO DEMOLISHING SATANIC FOUNDATIONS

1. My father, my God! The creator of all foundations, As I pray, I command every foundation that has been speaking against my life to open its ears and hear me tonight, you an evil foundation, open your ears and hear my voice in the mighty name of Jesus (Micah 6:2).

2. I know that you evil foundations are established through wickedness, therefore every wickedness I committed that satan used to build you wicked foundations, and I call upon the fire of God, as it came down during the time of Elijah to come down and consume you and lick you and your wickedness. I command the earth to open and swallow you as it happened to Korah, earth open and swallow them.

3. All satanic foundations, the high priest with your own arrows begin to fight amongst yourself, kill each other where ever you are operating from and die, die, die and never exist to the glory of God.

4. I bind you satan, I destroy you and I decree that every time you and your children mention my name you will receive thunder and lightning from your head to the sole of your feet.

5. Through the power of holiness and the fear of God in righteousness, I declare that a new godly, supernatural foundation is laid in my life in the mighty name of Jesus.

OVERTHROW EVIL GATES

- Let every gate anchoring bondage in my life catch fire and die.
- I command gates of righteousness to open over my life (Psalm; 118:19)
- I release supernatural battering rams against the gates of hell fighting against my life (Ezekiel 21:22)
- Tonight I rise up to possess the gates of my enemies
- I decree and declare that gates of hell cannot prevail against me (Mathew 16:18)

7. PRAYER FOR TEARING APART THE SATANIC ATMOSPHERE

- You satanic atmosphere created through false worship, satanic language, rumours, a spirit of division, prayerlessness, hypocrisy, evil speaking, be torn apart and never be mended, I command Holy Ghost fire to destroy you.
- You cloud of darkness hovering over my life, carrying false rain and deception, to mislead people against my life, hindering the glory of God to manifest in my life, I command the wind of God to drive you away to the Dead Sea, and never appear again.
- Father God, through the altar of true worship, passionate prayer, holiness and the altar of giving release a godly supernatural atmosphere over my life
- Father God, I decree that from tonight, I am I under a heavy, thick godly supernatural atmosphere.

8. PRAYER FOR ABUNDANCE AND UNLIMITED PROSPERITY

- Father, God, I decree that from today I will experience a season of unusual abundance, I decree that I shall never beg. I reject lack, insufficiency and scarcity in my life
  I command the release of all expectations of my life (finance, marriage, business, prosperity etc.).
- Father God, I ask you to release a supernatural atmosphere of increase upon my life
- Father God, I destroy every curse of poverty, lack, debts and scarcity in my life
- I declare and decree death overall spirits of cankerworms, palmerworms, caterpillars and locusts designed by satan to eat my blessings
- I decree and declare that this year 20____ is my year of abundance and unlimited prosperity.20____, the Lord has crowned you with goodness for my sake (Psalms 65:11)

9. PRAYER FOR UNCOMMON FAVOUR

- Lord, Jesus! Let your uncommon favour follow me and bring me greatness and divine elevation. Spirit of favour follows me all the days of my life.
- May the arrow of fire locate and destroy everything that stops favour from coming to me
- I decree that divine favour will come to me from everywhere.
- Father God! I declare that favour will pay all that I was to pay
- Father, make your face to shine upon me and be gracious unto me, lift up your countenance upon me and give me peace (Numbers 6:24 – 26

10. PRAYERS FOR DESTROYING DEMONIC COVENANTS

- I destroy all covenants, agreements and oaths that satan and his children made to destroy my life.
- I decree that my life shall not be destroyed, I command you destroyers to be destroyed.
- I separate and disconnect my life from all sins, covenants,

dedications, initiations and oaths of any person whom the devil ever used to pollute and destroy the foundation of my life.

☐ I destroy every blood covenant made by satan and his children, the altar where the sacrifice was done, catch fire and die.

☐ I pray for holiness and the fear of God in my life.

☐ I destroy and nullify spells, curses, evil prayers and enchantment made against my life.

☐ I decree and declare that there is no enchantment against my life.

PRACTICAL DISCIPLINES FOR COMING INTO THE PRESENCE OF GOD

1. Enter into your Secret chamber-The closet (be alone before God)
2. Kneel or lay prostrate in the Lord's presence.
3. Make your mind a sanctuary. Your mind is yours, make it obey.
4. Relax-be still-force yourself to be quiet
5. Fix your eyes on Jesus.
6. Take a few deep breaths.
7. Make sure your body and mind is into subjection

PRACTICAL WORSHIP STRATEGIES

- Read scriptures that exalt God.
- Sing songs to the Lord
- Exalt His name
- Remember His mighty works.
- Tell of His excellent greatness
- Acknowledge His sovereignty
- Physically express your worship and adorations.
- Worship with scriptures

(Psalms 111,112,113,117,134,144,145,147,148,149,150)

CHAPTER 6
ALPHA AND OMEGA PRAISE PRAISE HIS NAME THROUGH THE ALPHABET, FROM A TO Z

A-Alpha, Altogether lovely, Almighty God, Advocate, Author, Ancient of Days, Anchor

B-Bread, Balm of Gilead, Bright Morning Star, Beauty, Beginning, Best Gift, Branch, Bride

C-Creator, Captain, Comforter, Counsellor

D-Door, Defence, Deliverer, DayStar

E-Everlasting Father, Everything to me, Earnest of our inheritance

F-Faithful High priest, Father, a Friend of Sinners, Firstborn, Fairest of 10 000, First and last

G-God of All Comfort, Great God, Good Shepherd, Giver, Gift, Guide, Glory and Lifter of my head

H-Healer, Helper, Health, Holy One, Heir of all, High Priest, Hope of Ages

I-Immanuel, Invisible, Immortal, I AM

J-Judge, Jehovah, Jesus

K-King of Kings, King, Keeper

L-Lover of my soul, lord Strong and mighty, Lord, Lamb, Light of Life, Lilly of the valley

M-Maker, master, Marvellous One, Mighty God, Mediator

N-Never-failing God, Name above all names, Nest, New and living

O-Omnipotent, Omniscient, Omnipresent

P-Protector, Provider, Physician, Prince of Peace, My Peace, Passover, Priest forever, Promise

Q-Quickening One, Quickening Spirit, Quietness and My Confidence

R-Resurrection, Redeemer, Rock, Refuge, Righteousness One, My Righteousness

S-Saviour, Sanctifier, Sun, Shield, Shade, Shepherd, Sure, Shelter, Source

T-Teacher, Tower, Transformer, Truth

U-Unmovable, Unspeakable Gift, Upholder of all things

V-Victor, Vine, Vision

W-Water, Wonderful, Way, Wisdom, Worthy, Wing under which I trust

X-Excellent, Examiner of my heart, the ray of truth

Y-Yeshua, Yesterday, Today, Forever

Z-Zeal of Lord

ABOUT THE AUTHOR

Dr Sebenke Simon is a certified Neuro Linguistic Programming Practitioner (NLP) and a Life Coach. He has Master of Theology Degree (M.TH) and Doctorate Degree in Christian Education (D.CEd) from Grace International Bible University. He is a trained Christian Counsellor, he is also a Marriage Officer. He is the founder of Shalom Gospel Ministries, Rabonni International Bible College, Ablaze International Youth Club. He is the National Director of Grace International Bible University in Botswana.